Roots

GROWING DEEPER IN JESUS

Larry D. Metz, MA

TRILOGY CHRISTIAN PUBLISHERS
TUSTIN, CA

Trilogy Christian Publishers
A Wholly Owned Subsidiary of Trinity Broadcasting Network
2442 Michelle Drive
Tustin, CA 92780

Roots: Growing Deeper in Jesus

Cover design by Jeff Summers

For information, address Trilogy Christian Publishing

Rights Department, 2442 Michelle Drive, Tustin, Ca 92780.

Trilogy Christian Publishing/ TBN and colophon are trademarks of Trinity Broadcasting Network.

For information about special discounts for bulk purchases, please contact Trilogy Christian Publishing.

Manufactured in the United States of America

10 9 8 7 6 5 4 3 2 1

Library of Congress Cataloging-in-Publication Data is available.

ISBN 978-1-63769-096-3

ISBN 978-1-63769-097-0 (ebook)

Then Jesus came to them and said, "All authority in heaven and on earth has been given to me. Therefore go and make disciples of all nations, baptizing them in the name of the Father and of the Son and of the Holy Spirit, and teaching them to obey everything I have commanded you. And surely I am with you always, to the very end of the age."

Matthew 28:18-20

Blessed is the one
who does not walk in step with the wicked
or stand in the way that sinners take
or sit in the company of mockers,
but whose delight is in the law of the LORD,
and who meditates on his law day and night.
That person is like a tree planted by streams of water,
which yields its fruit in season
and whose leaf does not wither—
whatever they do prospers.

Psalm 1:1-3

Contents

Preface vii

Section One: Discipleship Overview 1

Introduction to Discipleship...................................2

The Three-Legged Stool 14

Developing the Inner Person 24

Me and My Neighbor 37

Doing Discipleship Differently 44

Section Two: Reading Your Bible Devotionally 59

Why Read the Bible?..60

What is the Bible?.. 68

Plan and Execute 79

What a Difference Culture Makes 93

Your Culture Versus God's Authority 145

Section Three: Relational Prayer 155

Catching Jesus Praying..156

Kingdom Relationship Brings Kingdom
    Direction..168

Models of Prayer for Every Need 177

God's Will Versus My Wants 185

Section Four: Not Without My Neigbor 193

Love and Solidarity 194

It is a Trinity 207

Roadside Repair When the Wheels Fall Off 225

Getting Across the Finish Line 235

Endnotes 242

Bibliography 243

Author Bio 250

Preface

You have waited all year for this. You scheduled your vacation with your boss. You've counted down the days. You have booked the hotels and your vacation destination. Today is Friday, and it is almost five o'clock. You look around. Your coworkers are clearing their desks for the weekend. Not you. You are clearing your desk for the week. You are leaving tomorrow for a one-week vacation. Tonight, you will finish packing so you can get an early start driving tomorrow. You can't wait to be a road warrior again!

It is Saturday evening when you pull into the hotel you booked. You are halfway to your destination. You will reach that Sunday afternoon. After checking in, you take your luggage to your room. The room is as spacious and clean as advertised. Before you leave the hotel to get a bite to eat, you decide to arrange your belongings. Upon taking inventory of your toiletries, you discover that you left your toothpaste at home. The hotel anticipated this. There, by the sink, is a small sign that reads, "Welcome to our hotel. If you forgot something, please visit the front desk. We will be glad to assist you with a free sample." Your heart rate slows as your anxiety vanishes. All is not lost. This is going to be a good trip after all!

There are times in life when we realize we are missing something. We don't have everything we are used to having. In these situations, it is important that we get everything we need. When push comes to shove, we might be able to do without a few things and still enjoy the journey. There are other things, however, that are a necessity. This is especially true when it comes to the Christian journey we call discipleship.

For many Christians outside the United States, being a Jesus-follower is a matter of life and death. Many countries around the world make it illegal to have open Christian gatherings. How can Christians grow their faith in these countries where they are prevented from openly worshiping God and expressing their faith?

The global pandemic of COVID-19 forced many churches across America to limit church attendance or close their doors for public health reasons. Suddenly, for American Christians, the main source of their Christian growth was absent. How can an American Christian grow their faith when they can't attend church?

As you read this book, think of it as the hotel welcome sign beside the bathroom sink. You may not have everything you want, but you can get everything you need. In Matthew 22:36-40, Jesus referenced the two greatest commandments. Jesus spoke of loving God and loving our neighbor. What did He mean by that? This question will be answered in the book.

This book will explain the three essential elements of discipleship. You cannot do without these if you want to experience a successful Christian journey. First, we will examine how to read the Bible. Hearing God's perspective on life is an integral part of loving God. Second, we will talk about prayer. Prayer is our side of this dialog with God. God speaks to us through His Word, and we speak to God through prayer. Third, we will consider what it means to love our neighbor. Love is more than a feeling.

While you read this book, we want you to enjoy your stay. More importantly, we want to help you get on the road of your Christian journey. You will be in this book for a short visit. Your objective will be to use what you get here for the rest of your journey. These essentials are designed to keep you growing through every season of your life. They are the bedrock of your Christian faith. This is the stuff that will help you reach your destination in grand style!

Section One:

Discipleship Overview

Introduction to Discipleship

Welcome to the family! You are not here by accident. You are here by design, God's design. From the creation of the world, God began using what He created to teach us what our spiritual life is supposed to look like.

Romans 1:20: "For since the creation of the world God's invisible qualities—his eternal power and divine nature—have been clearly seen, being understood from what has been made, so that people are without excuse."

Here is a review of our Christian journey up to this point.

1. We cannot join God's family. We must be born into it.

   Now there was a Pharisee, a man named Nicodemus who was a member of the Jewish ruling council. He came to Jesus at night and said, "Rabbi, we know that you are a teacher who has come from God. For no one could perform the signs you are doing if God were not with him." Jesus replied, "Very truly I tell you, no one can see the kingdom of God unless they are born again.

John 3:1-3

2. When God brings us into His family, He does not do a remodel job. God does not merely patch and paint! We are a brand new building from the ground up with a new foundation.

1 Corinthians 3:10-11: "By the grace God has given me, I laid a foundation as a wise builder, and someone else is building on it. But each one should build with care. For no one can lay any foundation other than the one already laid, which is Jesus Christ."

2 Corinthians 5:17: "Therefore, if anyone is in Christ, the new creation has come: The old has gone, the new is here!"

3. When we come into God's family, we come to the starting point from which our Christian life grows. Salvation is not our destination. The "planting of the Lord" now needs careful attention. This is where Discipleship joins the party!

and provide for those who grieve in Zion—to bestow on them a crown of beauty instead of ashes, the oil of joy instead of mourning, and a garment of praise instead of a spirit of despair. They will be called oaks of righteousness, a planting of the LORD for the display of his splendor.

Isaiah 61:3

Notice in this verse that the whole intent of God's "planting" is not to make us great but rather to increase *God's* honor and reputation! God is great because of His work in us.

I am the true vine, and my Father is the gardener. He cuts off every branch in me that bears no fruit, while every branch that does bear fruit he prunes so that it will be even more fruitful. You are already clean because of the word I have spoken to you. Remain in me, as I also remain in you. No branch can bear fruit by itself; it must remain in the vine. Neither can you bear fruit unless you remain in me.

John 15:1-4

The transmission of family values helps create a sense of personal identity. When I was a boy, my father told me one day about my ancestry and how that influenced our family dynamic. I was told we came from German heritage. Germans were not slackers. They had a good work ethic and took pride in their work. My father's instruction pointed me toward diligence and excellence.

In the same way, the Bible points us in the direction we are to go. We have not been saved to coast through life aimlessly. We have been saved to put our shoulders to the wheel, to apply the discipline learned through discipleship so that Jesus and the Father can be glorified.

Ephesians 2:10: "For we are God's handiwork, created in Christ Jesus to do good works, which God prepared in advance for us to do."

Are you aware that salvation (what many Christians refer to as being "born again") is not our destiny? Salvation is not the finish line. There is another destination to which we are traveling.

1. We are "created in Christ Jesus for good works" (Ephesians 2:10). Our good behavior does not bring us into God's kingdom. We have nothing to do with our birth into God's kingdom. Only God has control of that. Good behavior ("good works") is the direct result of the nature of a

good God who lives in us after we are born into God's kingdom.

2. There is a destiny that God points all His children to. The destiny to which we are traveling is transformation into the likeness of Jesus Christ (Romans 12:1-2; 2 Corinthians 3:18).

> Therefore, I urge you, brothers and sisters, in view of God's mercy, to offer your bodies as a living sacrifice, holy and pleasing to God— this is your true and proper worship. Do not conform to the pattern of this world, but be transformed by the renewing of your mind. Then you will be able to test and approve what God's will is—his good, pleasing and perfect will.
>
> Romans 12:1-2

2 Corinthians 3:18: "And we all, who with unveiled faces contemplate the Lord's glory, are being transformed into his image with ever-increasing glory, which comes from the Lord, who is the Spirit."

There are no slackers in God's family. In God's family, everybody pitches in. Unfortunately for me, during my growing-up years, my parents had hired help in the house. Other than learning to bake bread for the family, I did not have any assigned chores. Since I never really learned to pull my weight in the family, this attitude toward discipleship was difficult for me to grasp.

The economic engine of a large family runs well because everyone is expected to contribute to the well-being of the family. Every individual has a duty in keeping with his or her age and ability. This is the way it is in God's family (the Family of Christians). As an aside, this is also the way it is in the gathering of like-minded believers in a local church.

The apostle Paul likened the worldwide community of believers to a body (1 Corinthians 12:12-30). A human body is an integrated and interdependent sum of many parts. All these parts, both seen and unseen, derive their reason for being and independent direction from the head. Not all members function at the same rate of intensity or carry the same job description. But each member is vitally important to the health of the whole body. If the head is ever separated from the body, the body dies. If one member of the body is wounded, aid and healing are rushed to that member. If one member stops working up to factory specifications, the body becomes ill and needs downtime until that member recovers. If a member is separated from the body through surgery, that member is considered dead as far as that body is concerned.

The theme of the body in the New Testament underscores the importance of the theme of one's neighbor found in the Old Testament. From the early pages of the Old Testament to the final chapter of the New Testament, this recurring emphasis continually bubbles to the surface like water in an Artesian well. In our modern setting, we might express this priority emphatically. When asked, "Are you ready to proceed?" we would exclaim, "Not without my neighbor!"

When the going gets tough, it helps to have a traveling companion. Discipleship is more about the community than it is about the individual. One objection might be, "How will I get my needs met if I'm always looking out for the needs of somebody else?" That is a good question.

1. When I am in community and looking out for the needs of others, those other people that I am interdependent with are also looking out for my needs.

2. I am not supposed to be able to solve my problems by myself. Success through individual accomplishment is the fertile soil that produces pride. If I want God's help, I must continually work to rid my life of pride. This means staying in fellowship with other believers and letting them help me with my struggles. A good verse to remember is James 4:6, "But he gives us more grace. That is why Scripture says: "God opposes

the proud but shows favor to the humble" (see also Psalm 138:6, Proverbs 3:34, Matthew 23:12, and 1 Peter 5:5).

3. Helpful traveling companions (other disciples of Jesus) are meant to offer me a visible reminder of a spiritual truth. I am dependent on Someone else for kingdom life. Remember: "For it is by grace you have been saved, through faith—and this is not from yourselves, it is the gift of God— not by works, so that no one can boast" (Ephesians 2:8-9).

I needed someone else (Jesus) to birth me into God's kingdom. As I needed help there, I need help all along the way to grow in Christ. I cannot reach my destination by myself.

When I become a disciple of Jesus Christ, God uses me to create an ongoing legacy. As I am being discipled, I am to disciple others. This does not mean that I have all the answers. Far from it! This only means that as I am discovering spiritual food that nourishes my soul, I am to pass that food on to my fellow travelers so that they, too, can grow in their faith. Spiritual food creates life in every individual to which it is given.

1. The feeding of the five thousand recorded in Matthew 14, Mark 6, and Luke 9 is a visible ex-

ample of how discipleship is intended to work. Jesus gave bread to his disciples. They took the pieces and gave them to the people. The bread and fish did not stop feeding people until every need was met. When the hunger of the crowd was satisfied, the disciples were instructed to pick up the remainder. There were twelve baskets of fragments remaining.

2. Jesus commissioned His disciples when He spoke the following to them: "Again Jesus said, 'Peace be with you! As the Father has sent me, I am sending you'" (John 20:21). Jesus clarified His disciples' mission when he gave them the commandment recorded by Matthew:

Then the eleven disciples went to Galilee, to the mountain where Jesus had told them to go. When they saw him, they worshiped him; but some doubted. Then Jesus came to them and said, "All authority in heaven and on earth has been given to me. Therefore go and make disciples of all nations, baptizing them in the name of the Father and of the Son and of the Holy Spirit, and teaching them to obey everything I have commanded you. And surely I am with you always, to the very end of the age."

Matthew 28:16-20

The disciples' mission was to replicate the disciple-making process He had begun with them. Disciple-making was to be an ongoing legacy of these followers of Jesus.

Every race has a finish line. In discipleship, our Christian journey, where is the tape? How do we know when we have completed our mission? Is it when all the world has heard the message of salvation through TV or radio? Is it when multitudes commit their lives to Christ at the end of a gospel presentation? Have we successfully completed our mission then? Have we earned a rest?

Jesus never commanded us to make converts. He commanded us to make disciples. At a spiritual conversion, a person arrives at the starting point, not the finish line. Conversion is where the journey begins. Conversion is where a person's real spiritual work starts. Let me illustrate.

When a person wants to drive to an unknown destination, a navigation aid is often used. This navigation aid can come as one of the options on a vehicle. Many people use an app on their phones to guide them. Every navigation aid works the same way. You either type or speak your destination. The navigation aid computes the best route to the destination, and you are on your way. There is one catch, however. The navigation aid will not work unless you allow it to discover your starting position. Only when your starting location is established can the best route to the destination be calculated.

Spiritual conversion is to a disciple what the starting location is to a navigation aid. So, if conversion is the starting point, what is the destination?

Romans 8:29: "For those God foreknew he also predestined to be conformed to the image of his Son, that he might be the firstborn among many brothers and sisters."

Notice the word "predestined" in Romans 8:29. There is a close connection between "predestined" and *destination!* A Christian's final destination is conformity into the image of (or growth into the character traits of) Jesus.

Discipleship, then, is the journey between spiritual conversion and our destination.

Questions for Group Reflection

1. Reflect on your Christian journey to this point. What were you taught in your Christian circle about how to become a Christian? What different messages have you heard from other groups?

2. People in today's world claim there are many ways to get to God. Read what Jesus said about this in John 14:6. How does this "exclusive" message of Christianity compare to other religions of the world?

3. When you became a Christian, what were you told about your destiny? What was it, and how does that compare to what you read in this chapter about your destiny?

4. If you attend a church, consider the message you hear about getting involved. What is "Christian work" as defined by your group? How does the message you heard compare to what you read about everybody pitching in? What is the focus in that section?

5. Every group of people experiences a conflict at some point. This happens in marriages, small groups, and larger church groups. How do many people handle conflict in a group setting? How does this compare to what you read in the section, "When the Going Gets Tough?"

13

The Three-Legged Stool

When I am on the move and want a quick rest from walking on rugged terrain, a folding three-legged stool can't be beat. Its three points on the ground distribute weight evenly, giving my legs a welcome break.

Granted, the even terrain of a campsite offers one the luxury of lounging in a four-legged chair with a back. A four-legged chair (four points on the ground) is fine as long as the ground cooperates. The same concept holds true at home. Put a four-legged "anything" down on the floor. If you expect stability with no wobble, the floor had better be flat. This applies to a chair, a table, or the workbench in your shop. If the floor does not cooperate, you will be forever trimming legs or inserting wedges just to get rid of that frustrating wobble!

But there is no problem with the three-legged stool. It is just happy to accommodate with a comfortable respite when the need arises. Stability does not depend on the ground surface. There may be branches, debris, and rocks on the surface. It does not matter. The very things that wreak havoc on a four-legged chair are a cinch for a three-legged stool. The stool thrives under these less-than-ideal conditions. It meets the challenge of the terrain and offers the necessary stability and rest in the time of need.

Our three points of discipleship are similar to a three-legged stool. They give a lot of stability in rough terrain. Understanding that, we must now examine the process of discipleship. How does a person live the life of a disciple, a learner?

A disciple is a learner bound for a destination. Every disciple wants the product, that worthwhile destination at the end of the trip. The non-negotiable part of this is the price a person must pay to get what he or she wants. The process of discipleship instruction is necessary if one wants to be conformed into the likeness of Jesus. Since the disciple values this destination above all else, the required discipline found within the instruction can be endured. The discipline is what enables the disciple to reach the desired end.

The desired end has boundaries and structure into which only a well-trained student can fit. The undisciplined will not make it. They have too much baggage. They have ways and means of being and behaving that are beneath the level of the destination. Sloppiness and immaturity do not cut it at the level of this desired end point. There is a code of conduct to be learned. There are levels of performance to be achieved. There, certainly, are things to be learned, things to be endured, and things to be discarded.

Discipline is one of the things that sets a civilian apart from someone in the military. If a person enlists or is drafted into the military, the objective of the military is a person with a certain skill set and mental attitude. How does a civilian achieve the military's target? One word: boot camp. Boot camp is designed to instill an individual with the necessary skills to fight and survive on the field of battle. These skills are instilled using instruction, discipline, correction, and submission to authority.

How does this apply to Christian discipleship? When God delivers a person out of the power of darkness and places that person into the kingdom of His Son Jesus (Colossians 1:13), that person has a stated objective. The objective of this person is to be conformed into the image (profile, likeness, resemblance) of Jesus Christ (Romans 8:29). This is all in keeping with what Jesus said a disciple was to become. Jesus advocated the common Jewish understanding of His day when He said that a student would become like his teacher (Matthew 10:25).

When a person becomes a Christian, there are ways of being, believing, and behaving that have to go. They do not fit with the high calling of the stated objective. Many things have to be unlearned, while other things have to be learned.

Military "Basic" (boot camp) usually lasts six weeks. The disciple of Jesus has no such luck. Discipleship for a Christian is a life-long experience. There are always new things to learn and new ways to encounter our culture as we are conformed (formed together, fashioned, adjusted, shaped) into the image of Jesus.

The process of discipleship is a life-long experience of instruction, discipline, and submission to authority. This is the way God has chosen to get us from where He found us to where He wants us to be.

The process of discipleship is the normal existence of every follower of Jesus. Discipleship is not something reserved for the "saint" or the "super-Christian." Christian discipleship is normal Christianity, and normal Christianity involves lifelong discipleship. If a person does not want to be a disciple, then they cannot be a Christian.

Jesus did not tell His disciples to make converts out of everyone and disciples out of only a few of those converts. Jesus never told His disciples to make converts. Jesus said: "Therefore go and make disciples of all nations, baptizing them in the name of the Father and of the Son and of the Holy Spirit" (Matthew 28:19).

Conversion is supposed to be a means to an end. In other words, a person must experience conversion in order to start on the path of discipleship. God's plan (God's end) is always the transformation into the image of Jesus through the training and discipline of discipleship.

If a person, then, is to pursue discipleship to Jesus, what makes for a Christian's "Basic" training?

Within "classical" (early) Christian circles, there were many disciplines Christians used to grow deeper into Christ. These disciplines are very useful in weaning a person away from dependence on this present world (the created order). For many people today, however, adding disciplines may have the same effect as adding additional legs to a stool. Life can become cumbersome and unwieldy in many of the life stages where we find ourselves.

There are three essential disciplines that can make for a very stable Christian life in difficult times. When life gets tough and the going gets hard, we all need something secure we can depend on. We need something that can offer rest to our weary souls. What we need is the three-legged stool of discipleship.

The three essential elements all disciples need to work into their lives are (in order of importance):

1. daily Bible reading,

2. daily prayer, and

3. daily loving (attaching one's self to) one's neighbor.

I will go into more detail on each of these later, but here is a summary of these basic "legs" and why these elements are ranked in this order.

1. *The Bible* is God's primary instruction manual that teaches us how to properly relate to God, our world, and each other. It reveals God's character and nature to us and tells us what God's will is for us. Since God spoke this universe and world into existence, we understand that God's Word is a tangible expression of His vested authority (Isaiah 55:10-11). Therefore, when we read the Bible, we do so not because that is "what a Christian is supposed to do." First on every Christian's agenda must be to come fully under the lordship and authority of Jesus Christ. We read the Bible in order to place ourselves fully under God's authority. Living under God's authority is the foundational cornerstone that supports all our Christian life in the kingdom of God.

2. *Prayer* has been summarized as "talking to God." This is partially true. Prayer is supposed to be a dialogue with God. If I have a conversation with

someone and I do all the talking, I am not having a conversation. I am having a monologue, and the other person is having an exercise in listening. In contrast to a monologue, a dialogue is where both parties take turns speaking and listening. (Maybe that is why God gave me two ears and only one mouth!) In prayer, I will do some talking but normally seek to do a lot of listening. When I am reading the Bible, I am prayerfully reading the Bible. I am engaged with what I am reading because I really want to "hear what the Spirit is saying" to me, a part of God's universal church (Revelation 2:7). Second on every Christian's agenda must be to seek God's face. We seek His face in order to know Him and so that we might hear His instructions so that we can fulfill His will. When we live under God's authority, our first response should be to heartily obey whatever God tells us in prayer if what He says requires a response from us.

3. *Loving my neighbor* does not mean I must feel good about my neighbor all the time. It does mean that I am to attach myself to and stand in solidarity with my neighbor. If you want more specifics quickly, read through 1 Corinthians 13. This is a chapter in the New Testament where the apostle Paul lays out in greater detail what

the practice of love looks like. This is one chapter in the Bible that moves this concept "Loving my Neighbor" from a feeling into specific behaviors that will benefit another person that God has placed close to me. In the beginning (Genesis 1-2), God put man in a garden and in relationship with another human being. God has tasked man with managing his world and managing his relationships. Third on every Christian's agenda must be to care for his relationships. When Christians distance themselves from (or hate) other Christians close to them, they inadvertently cut their lifeline to their Creator. It is especially true when the relationship break comes as the result of differences in preference. If a person wants to repair his relationship with God, he must do everything he can to repair his relationship with his neighbor.

The terrain of life is often rugged and rocky. Things surprise us. We are not expecting financial reversal, devastating illness, or even broken relationships. Suddenly, we find ourselves dealing with them. When life is hard and rugged, we need good support that can stabilize us. We need Basic Discipleship. We need the three-legged stool of Christian disciplines. When we have these, we will be traveling light over life's tough terrain. We will be growing in our likeness to Jesus, and we will be bringing glory to the Father in the darkest of times.

Questions for Group Reflection

1. Consider what you have heard about how to follow Jesus daily. How is that message similar or different from the discussion of Discipleship in this chapter?

2. When it comes to growing your faith, what have you been taught about how to grow your faith? How does that compare with the structure presented in this chapter?

3. Internal guilt is a big motivator in American culture. When you think about your own track record of prayer and Bible reading, what kind of feelings start bubbling up on the inside? Now read Romans 8:1. What does this verse do for those feelings?

4. When we think about doing a good job, we typically think in terms of performance. When a person wants to continue working at a job, they hope for a good performance evaluation at the end of the year. Read Ephesians 2:8 and Colossians 2:20-23. What do these verses say about the part performance plays in receiving salvation and keeping (or tending to) our salvation after we come into God's family?

Developing the Inner Person

One of the weaknesses of twentieth-century American Christianity has been the practice of making individual Christians dependent on the local church for just about everything.

Here are some assumptions I have gleaned from my conversations with many American Christians. These may or may not be prevalent in American Christianity when you read this. See if you recognize any of these.

1. If you want to learn about the Bible, you must attend a local church or listen to a preacher on the radio or television. They are the ones who have received specialized Bible training. They are the Bible scholars. Therefore, they are the only ones qualified to tell people about the Bible.

2. If you want to expand the kingdom of God, you invite people to church to hear the pastor. If a

special evangelist comes to the local church or comes to the city for a city-wide crusade, you invite people to hear the evangelist. These ministers are called evangelists because God had given them the special job of explaining the good news of the kingdom of God (the Gospel) to people in such a way that they want to be converted.

3. Church work (the Lord's work) is always tied somehow to the local church. There seems to be a wall of separation between where God lives (at church) and His work happens versus where the individual Christian lives and where he or she works five or six days out of the week. There are workdays, and then there is the Lord's day.

Here are some assumptions I have gleaned from my conversations with (or listening to) many American pastors. These may or may not be prevalent in American Christianity when you read this. See if you recognize any of these.

1. If people are going to learn about the Bible, they need to come to church. That means the pastor, in order to succeed, must make ministry his or her only vocation. After all, if the pastor does not preach well, the people will not come, and therefore they will not grow in their faith. If the pastor

does not prepare well, the people will not learn and so will not grow in their faith. If the people do not grow in their faith, God will hold the pastor personally responsible.

2. If you want to expand the kingdom of God, you must grow your local congregation. The pastor, as the main spokesman for the church, has the delegated responsibility to contact people in their homes or businesses and explain the good news of the kingdom of God (the Gospel). After all, that is what the people in the pew are paying him to do. (This model used to determine church success is a business model. In other words, if the numbers of conversions (sales) increase and finances increase, then the church—and pastor—are a success. I do not believe this model of determining success is one that Jesus would recognize, much less approve of.)

3. The church building is where the Lord's work happens. Therefore, we must recruit greeters, ushers, Sunday school teachers, children's workers, and youth workers. If people are not involved in the local church when the doors are open, the Lord's work is not happening. The pastor does the Lord's work seven days a week while the congregation does their own work five or six days out of the week. Then, they all engage in the

Lord's work at church. After all, there are work-days, and then there is the Lord's day.

I hope you have noticed a similarity between the viewpoints of American Christianity shared by (1) the people of the pew and (2) the people of the pulpit. In fact, I just gave you the answer in the way I described all these people. I described them in terms of pew and pulpit.

American Christianity, by and large, has been centered and focused on church buildings. This has been the main weakness of the culture of American Christianity. Why do I call this a weakness? It is because one must seriously consider in the current American church culture whether Christians would have what they needed if suddenly church buildings were closed or attendance was restricted. All Christians must learn how to feed themselves. It is we who must make disciples. Jesus went to the temple regularly, as did His disciples. Jesus' focus, however, was not on growing a greater temple. Jesus' focus was on growing big people.

There is a Navajo proverb I have heard since I was a youth. It goes like this: "Give a man a fish, and you feed him for a day. Teach a man to fish, and you feed him for a lifetime" (Quote Investigator).

If American Christians are going to thrive, not just survive, in difficult times, they must learn how to fish.

In other words, they must learn how to find spiritual food themselves. They must learn how to thrive by becoming God-centered rather than church-centered or pastor-centered. What do I mean?

1. They must learn through consistent practice and experience that they can reap a great benefit and grow their faith through personal daily Bible reading. I know. This might make many pastors feel insecure. After all, if people can hear from God personally, doesn't that make a pastor unnecessary? Not at all! Stay with me, and we will get to that!

2. They must learn to become Christ-focused. When a person is Christ-focused, they understand that the kingdom of God and His work are larger than any church or denomination. This big view will yield great results. When you look through the lens of a microscope, you can examine every part of your specimen (or your church). The problem with microscopic vision is that every flaw of the local church is magnified. Maybe that's why pastors must tolerate so much grumbling and complaining in a church. The people cannot see the Lord for looking at the flaws. Not only do they see the flaws of their own church, but then the microscopic lens is trained toward

another church down the street. Suddenly, God's kingdom and work become diminished by using this overriding microscopic focus.

3. They must learn how to tear down the invisible wall that separates the Lord's work on Sunday from secular work on weekdays. American Christians need to learn how to tear down that mental wall that divides their days between sacred and secular. American Christians have been indoctrinated with this mental divide between sacred and secular by the cultural offensive to establish the *separation of church and state*. As long as church and state remain separated, the Lord's work will only happen at the local church. But when that wall comes down, all of life will become sacred. When every day becomes sacred, the Lord's work will happen everywhere the Christian goes because the whole earth is "full of His glory" (Isaiah 6:3).

Remember when I mentioned the insecurity of some pastors earlier? A pastor need not feel insecure. There is plenty of work to do. This work can be divided into two categories. These categories are the Old Testament and the New Testament.

The Old Testament tells the story of the Levitical priest (comparable to today's pastor). God tasked the Levitical priests with the duties of the tabernacle (Numbers 1:53). We must remember, however, that the priest was also to be with the people because he was also tasked with teaching the people the difference between what was holy (what God accepted) and what was unholy (what God rejected; Ezekiel 44:23).

The New Testament (especially the Gospels) tells the story of Jesus teaching regular working people how to integrate their everyday work into God's kingdom work. The disciples were focused on the Sea of Galilee. Jesus focused their eyes on the nation of Israel and then on the nations of the World. When Jesus called them to be His disciples, they were using their skills to survive under the authority of the Romans. Jesus taught them to use their skills to thrive under the authority of God's kingdom. Jesus told his disciples that as they were going, they were to engage in the kingdom work of making disciples (Matthew 28:19).

To summarize, a pastor is an equipment manager. A pastor has charge of the supply room. When a Christian in the church is commissioned by the Lord to fulfill a task in the kingdom, that Christian should talk to the pastor if they do not readily have what they need. The pastor will determine the nature of the work and then help the Christian get the necessary tools to accomplish what the Lord commanded. This is the essence of Ephesians 4:11-13:

So Christ himself gave the apostles, the prophets, the evangelists, the pastors and teachers, to equip his people for works of service, so that the body of Christ may be built up until we all reach unity in the faith and in the knowledge of the Son of God and become mature, attaining to the whole measure of the fullness of Christ.

Ephesians 4:11-13

So, what is in this equipment room? Come! Examine this with me!

We are talking about developing the inner person in this segment. Why is that important? Why not focus on methods like evangelism, teaching, or counseling? Methods like evangelism, teaching, and counseling are important skill sets. Let me focus, for a moment, on where Jesus' focus was. Look at the following two verses:

Mark 3:14: "He appointed twelve that they might be with him and that he might send them out to preach."

On the last and greatest day of the festival, Jesus stood and said in a loud voice, "Let anyone who is thirsty come to me and drink. Whoever believes in me, as Scripture has said, rivers of living water will flow from within them."

By this he meant the Spirit, whom those who believed in him were later to receive. Up to that time the Spirit had not been given, since Jesus had not yet been glorified.

John 7:37-39

In Mark 3:14, we find Jesus' primary focus was on "being" ("be with Him") before "doing" ("send them out to preach"). If we are to disciple like Jesus discipled, we must concern ourselves with getting people into the habit of "being" with Jesus. Skill sets of evangelism, teaching, and counseling belong to the "doing" part that comes after the "being" part is developed. Remember, Jesus' disciples learned the skill sets of ministry while they were with Jesus, observing what He was doing.

In John 7:37-39, "rivers of living water" is the life of the Spirit that flows from the source of a person's "being" center. "Living" is the God-quality that enlivens the lifeless and stagnant. It is the God-breath that creates new substance from what has been long dead and decomposed (Ezekiel 37:1-10). It is the God-stream that guarantees both life and fruitfulness in an otherwise chaotic place (Psalm 1:1-6).

What are some of the tools that help a person learn to "be" with Jesus? I am indebted to Richard J. Foster for the following list. This list is wonderfully explained in his book, *Celebration of Discipline, The Path to Spiritual Growth* (HarperCollins Publishers, 1978). I will just note these disciplines as Foster lists them in his table of contents.

> The Inward Disciplines
> Meditation
> Prayer (*discussed in this work as Prayer*)
> Fasting
> Study (*discussed in this work as daily Bible reading*)
> The Outward Disciplines
> Simplicity
> Solitude
> Submission
> Service

Foster discusses these Outward disciplines in terms of how we relate to those closest to us, our neighbor. I will offer a different perspective of relating to one's neighbor. I highly recommend Foster's perspective as these disciplines work to wean us away from our reliance on this world, this created order, so that we can put our reliance on God.

> The Corporate Disciplines
> Confession
> Worship
> Guidance
> Celebration

This listing of twelve disciplines by Richard Foster includes material discussed in this book. This book will treat Foster's discussions on Prayer and Study, however, in a different manner. While Foster's book touches on themes included in this work, his book goes beyond the scope of this writing.

It is my intent to provide a Christian in a local church the essentials, three basic Christian disciplines, that can move a person out of the starting blocks of conversion and onto a solid path of relationship with Jesus. These three essential disciplines will enable a Christian to nourish their spiritual life so that they can grow deeper in Jesus even when church attendance is not possible. After a person is solidly implementing the basic disciplines, these additional disciplines Richard Foster discusses are well worth a Christian's time and attention.

Questions for Group Reflection

1. Think about what you read in this chapter. When it comes to you growing deeper in Jesus, what do you feel are the strengths and weaknesses of the American church culture?

2. The COVID-19 pandemic was discovered in China in December 2019 and quickly spread to countries all around the world. As a result, many churches in the United States were forced to either cancel church services or severely restrict attendance. How did this interruption in church attendance affect your ability to grow your faith effectively away from your church group?

3. Read Matthew 16:18. Who is talking here? What do you think is the "church" He is referring to? How does this verse compare to the culture of American Christianity today?

4. In church, a lot is said about skill sets. These are things like learning how to share our faith with non-Christians and learning how to lead a small group Bible Study in a Christian setting. Consider Mark 3:14. Why do you think "being with Jesus" was such a big deal with Jesus? Isn't that wasting time?

5. How did you feel when you read the list of disciplines outlined by Richard Foster? What do you

think about the value of beginning a structured discipleship program with something simple before working toward something more complex later?

Me and My Neighbor

Throughout the Bible, the theme of "Me and My Neighbor" (this value of relational living) is a reoccurring subject.

The Torah (Law/Instruction)

Genesis: God creates Man in and for relationship, but Cain cuts off his relationship with his brother Abel. By extension, he also cuts off his relationship with God.

Exodus: Love God, and love your neighbor (Exodus 20, Ten Commandments).

Leviticus: How to live with God and my neighbor (Leviticus 19).

Numbers: The record of traveling in the wilderness for forty years, with a census at the beginning and end of the journey. Numbers recounts how this "neighbor" thing worked out in everyday life.

Deuteronomy: A rehearsal of God's Torah (instruction), with a charge to take the land together. The tribes were to work together, not individually.

History

Joshua, Judges, Ruth, 1 & 2 Samuel, 1 & 2 Kings, 1 & 2 Chronicles, Ezra, Nehemiah, Esther: These books record how people lived out life with their neighbors. They record both the successes and failures and how God responded to each.

Poetry and Wisdom

Job, Psalms, Proverbs, Ecclesiastes, Song of Solomon: These books offer counsel on living in community with my neighbor in a way that God approves.

Major Prophets

Isaiah, Jeremiah, Lamentations, Ezekiel, Daniel: considered "major" because they contain a large amount of text (the books are long) (Rose Publishing). These prophets were warning God's people to stop abusing their neighbors. If they did not, God would defend the abused by removing the abusers from the land. You will also read here, "The reason why you have been removed is because you abused your neighbor."

Minor Prophets

Hosea, Joel, Amos, Obadiah, Jonah, Micah, Nahum, Habakkuk, Zephaniah, Haggai, Zechariah, Malachi: considered "minor" because they contain a small amount of text (the books are short) (Rose Publishing). Like the major prophets, these prophets either foretold disaster before captivity or explained why the disaster happened during captivity. Their theme was, "This will be/was God's response to abusing your neighbor."

Gospels

Matthew, Mark, Luke, & John: the record of how God joined mankind in community and for relationship by taking on human flesh. They also record how Jesus died for his "neighbor" (mankind), removing the barrier of sin that kept mankind from enjoying the relationship with God the Creator.

Acts

Acts: the historical record of the creation of a new band of Jesus' followers calling themselves "The Way." Acts also records the Jewish resistance movement against "The Way." This resistance was an effort to stamp out a movement that appeared threatening to the Jewish nation.

Epistles

Romans, 1 & 2 Corinthians, Galatians, Ephesians, Philippians, Colossians, 1 & 2 Thessalonians, 1 & 2 Timothy, Titus, Philemon, Hebrews, James, 1 & 2 Peter, 1, 2 & 3 John, Jude: these books were written to (1) communities of Jesus' followers that were established in various cities as recorded in the Book of Acts, and (2) leaders of or individuals within these communities. Two outside forces threatened the stability of these first-century churches. These forces were the teachings of Gnosticism as well as Judaizers who tried to turn Christians from faith in Christ back to obedience to the Law of Moses. These letters (Epistles) advise either (1) how the people of "The Way" were to relate to each other within their group, or (2) how they were to respond to the Jewish resistance movement and Gnostic teachings outside their group.

Revelation

Revelation: Bible scholars typically view Revelation as a chronology of end-time events. Seen through the lens of relationships, however, we observe God making the final division of mankind between those in relationship with Him and those not in relationship with Him. In this division, man is treated as a person of relationship, not as an isolated individual.

Man lives in community in this world before his God. God reflects toward mankind a generous and compassionate attitude. Man (for all practical purposes) is God's "neighbor" (Genesis 1:26). As a reflection of his Creator, man is charged with reflecting a generous and compassionate attitude toward his neighbor, his fellowman.

The Old Testament position was that when a man acted justly (generously and compassionately) toward his neighbor, even in the face of receiving injustice, God counted the man's actions as righteousness.

In the New Testament, when God removed our sin barrier by the blood of Jesus (Romans 5), He made it possible for us to behave through the enablement of His nature in a generous and compassionate way toward our neighbor (Romans 6).

If I am to be a disciple of Jesus Christ and walk before Him as He desires, I must pay attention to who walks beside me. Being a Christian is not about just "me and Jesus." I hurt Jesus when I hurt others He loves (Acts 26:9-15). I experience God's light when I respond to others with compassion.

Questions for Group Reflection

1. Think about what you read in this chapter. When it comes to you growing deeper in Jesus, what do you feel are the strengths and weaknesses of the American church culture?
2. Read Matthew 5:20 and compare that to Romans 3:21-22. What do you think is meant by the word "righteousness" in these two verses?
3. How do you think these two verses square with the Old Testament understanding of "righteousness?"
4. We often think of the cross of Jesus. The Roman cross was made up of two members. There was a vertical (up-and-down) member attached to a horizontal (right-and-left) member. If we consider that the vertical member symbolizes our relationship with God, what do you think the horizontal member might represent? Why do you think that is important?

Doing Discipleship Differently

I was born in the middle of the twentieth century. The 1950s and 1960s were an interesting time to come of age both overseas and in the United States. Having been raised by missionary parents overseas in West Africa, I was constantly exposed to the evangelism (getting new converts) side of Christianity. That was the main thrust of missionary work overseas. It was also what I was exposed to in the American churches I visited.

My parents did focus on education overseas. They realized early in their missionary career that local people who were immersed in the local culture and customs were more effective in evangelism than outsiders. So even though they trained local converts how to become pastors, the overall focus of ministry appeared to rest on evangelism, gaining new converts into Christianity. If you have ever observed the activity of a hive, you will have noticed that bees work hard at gathering nectar to make honey. In my early exposure to church life overseas, there always seemed to be a hive of activity involving gathering converts. These West African people were primarily illiterate. Since they could not read, they could not develop a systematic discipleship program available to a literate culture like Americans. The best they could do was learn Bible stories by heart. This seemed to carry over into my early Christian training in my family of origin. I was not aware of much instruction regarding how to make progress in a personal discipleship program. While Bible stories were learned at church, I was not aware of how these stories could have practical application to living. For me, the Bible existed in a vacuum. There were Bible stories, and then there was everyday life.

The same appeared true in the American churches I had the privilege of observing when our family returned to the United States for a year of church visitation. This became especially apparent in the 1960s. First and foremost, the primary message delivered and received in churches was essentially, "get more converts, because Jesus might return at any moment." That message is accurate and is found in Scripture. The problem comes with focusing on that message specifically to the exclusion of a correlating emphasis on "what's next after conversion?" I never really heard in American churches how a Christian was to address the racial unrest of the

1960s. What I found interesting as a teenager was that an American church person would happily give money to a missionary going overseas to speak to people of other races. But that same person would not dream of crossing the street to speak to a racially different person in his own neighborhood. For some reason, the gospel wasn't penetrating the hearts of the American Jesus' followers I was exposed to. They appeared to be more "culture-followers" than "Jesus-followers."

Growing up in a missionary's home and being in churches my whole life gave me a good foundation of the basic Bible stories. I found, however, that as I matured physically, I was not maturing spiritually.

I remember my Junior or Senior year in high school when my mother began an intensive study program on basic cooking, laundry, ironing, and elementary sewing (reattaching buttons) skills. I had a crash course on the skills I would need to handle life on my own.

There was something lacking, however. While I was learning how to live independently from my nuclear family, nobody considered teaching me the skills I would need to make my faith my own. Yes, I had become a convert to Christianity. I had been converted to Christianity at the age of eight. But I was still a baby Christian as a teenager. I was wide open to the assaults of the adversary. Even though I knew Bible stories by heart, I had no clue how to grow my faith from there.

When I returned to the United States a year ahead of my parents to go to college, I found a church to attend and began attending. I observed that church life as a late teenager was the same as it had been during my formative years. The structure had not changed. There was Bible instruction (Sunday school) during the first hour. In this hour, the teacher had a lesson plan that he or she delivered. It was typically filled with Bible content and had little real-life application. Following Sunday school came a corporate worship time followed by preaching. Again, proclamation without feedback or discussion.

I drifted for years struggling in my faith until maybe my early-to-mid 40s. A church my wife and I attended began promoting reading through the Bible in a year. Up to that time, my Bible reading had been sporadic at best. I noticed, however, that when I began a regular and systematic Bible reading program, a shift began taking place internally. Something began happening spiritually. Still, the worship and especially the Sunday school culture stayed the same. We were attending a church where expository Bible teaching and preaching was the norm. There was no lack of great Bible teaching. Still, it was an instruction model where one person stood or sat at the front, and everybody in attendance listened and took notes. There was little feedback opportunity. There certainly was not much opportunity to put principles learned into practice in the community. Nobody reported on their experiences so they could learn from their successes and failures.

It was not until later in life, after having reached the end of a career in business, that I had the opportunity to train for a different area of ministry. My college and graduate school training had given me the degrees necessary for a career in full-time church ministry. Pulpit ministry never materialized like I thought it would. Business came to the rescue, helping put food on the table. Now that business opportunities vanished, I was left wondering how God wanted to use me in His kingdom. Somebody suggested chaplaincy training, and it was there that I began to learn how to do discipleship differently.

When I went into chaplaincy training, I expected it to duplicate the teaching model I had become so accustomed to. I was in training to be a hospital chaplain. I expected my trainers to teach me how to do a "proper" hospital visit. Was I ever in for a surprise! That was not what happened at all!

As I and my fellow chaplaincy interns discovered, what we had been accustomed to in all our educational learning was what may be called "pedagogy." Pedagogy can also be called "child learning." In pedagogy, the teacher or instructor sets the agenda, the students learn, absorb the instruction, maybe take a few exams, and then leave having "learned" something. Maybe the student would be fortunate enough to earn a certificate of completion, a diploma, or a degree. Chaplaincy training was really different!

Our trainers told us that this model of training would be called "andragogy." Andragogy can also be called "adult learning." Yes, there is instruction. However, the instruction is not task-specific. The instruction received is more about character formation. When it would come to the time to do the actual hospital visits, we would learn using the model, "Action–Reflection–Action."

I still remember the shock of the first session as a hospital chaplain intern. We were all handed books from which we would do readings. We listened in our first session about what it meant to be a hospital chaplain and began studying the character qualities of a chaplain. At this point, everything was fine. I was in familiar territory. I knew what to do with this. I was "learning" (or so I thought).

When the end of the first session came, our trainer informed us, "Well, that's all for today." And then came the "cold-water" directive, "Go do your hospital visits." I was suddenly terrified. Something was missing! Our instructor had failed to tell us how to do a hospital visit!

After the session was over, I approached the instructor to inform him of the missing information. The conversation went sort of like this:

"Uh, you told us to go do our hospital visitations. I do not know how to do a hospital visitation. You didn't tell us."

"Well, just go do one [Action]. We will get together in our next session and talk about it [Reflection]. Then you will have something to work with for your visits after the next session [Next Action]."

I persisted, "But how do you do a hospital visit? I don't know how!"

He remarked, "Just go do the best you can, and we'll talk about it. Just do something. Go talk to people, and then we'll talk about your experience."

Knowing that I was getting nowhere with this trainer, I went off to do my hospital "visitations." I had no idea what I was doing! All I did was talk to patients, families, and staff members. Little did I know how much learning would happen during this course of training!

When we returned for our next session, we learned how to take a visit and break it down:

- "What did we notice when we entered the room?"
- "What was the condition of the patient?"
- "Were there any family members present? What about hospital staff?"
- "Now, detail your conversation with the patient, family, and staff (who said what)."

- "How did you end the visit?"

After the chaplain interns and instructor had reviewed a visit, then the reflection began:

- "You didn't mention whether there were any cards or flowers in the room. What about those?"
- "Why did you respond to the patient initially like you did? Why do you think you felt those feelings?"
- "You said 'this' or 'that' to the family member or staff. I'm wondering if you considered saying something like 'xxx.'"
- "What during the visit made you choose that particular ending? Maybe in the future, you might consider 'xxx' in this situation. It might be more effective because of 'xxx.'"

There was something about this non-shaming, caring, close-quarter sharing that ignited a fire on the inside. I was not learning from just the instructor. Everybody was my teacher! While the chaplaincy instructor certainly had input, he did not need to have all the answers. But where the instructor did not have an answer I needed, someone else in the class did.

Suddenly I had a room full of resources. I noticed that my interior growth began accelerating. I became interconnected and interdependent with my fellow interns. My confidence grew, and (again) I entered a new phase of spiritual growth.

Reflecting on the positive experience I had with the andragogy model of learning in chaplaincy training, I have thought much about the pedagogy model of learning currently used in discipleship training. I wonder what would happen if we started doing discipleship differently? Maybe our discipleship would end up looking more like the model Jesus used:

- Jesus' teaching was about "being" and the attitudes toward life he possessed.
- Two different times he sent the disciples out to interact with their communities: first, it was the twelve, and then it was the seventy or seventy-two.
- After their interaction, the disciples came back to Jesus, and they talked about it.

Remember, it was these men that ended up shaking their world!

What might a typical discipleship class look like using an andragogy model?

- Class instruction would focus on

o "being" principles and attitudes common to a person living as a "Jesus' follower";

o how to use the basic tools that will support our inner spiritual "being" in Christ Jesus.

- Encourage the class members to interact with their neighbors. Remember, we are not talking about going door-to-door in the neighborhood. We are talking about viewing all of life as sacred. That means I speak, listen, and respond at the grocery store, doctor's office, car dealership, mechanic, or neighbor while I am walking in the neighborhood. I am also interacting with my wife and children inside the walls of my home. Basically, I understand that all my living is done in "sacred space." Wouldn't that understanding revolutionize how we conduct our affairs?

- In the next class session, we would:
  o review/discuss an interaction(s),
  o instruct on more "being" principles,
  o review/discuss basic tool usage (difficulties/ successes) we encountered.

The "Rabbi/disciple" training model that Jesus used was a Middle Eastern model common to His era. It was not a Western model of learning. The Western teaching method is a method that is largely a pedagogical method. A teacher tells what the students are expected to learn. There is little review or discussion. The method Jesus used had plenty of "telling." Jesus was always telling somebody something they needed to hear. The difference, I feel, in Jesus' method was that it was more andragogical than the Western method. There was more opportunity for reflection built in. The parables were all about reflection. One listened to the parables, saw themselves in the narrative, and drew a conclusion. Jesus' parables brought people to a crisis point in their lives. They had to decide before God and their neighbor whether they would begin living life differently. Many times, the parable narrative provided a dire warning of what was to come if a person did not change direction.

The advantage of "child learning" (pedagogy) is that it can fit into a specific time slot. The teacher has control and can start and stop at will. Instructor-led teaching may include a challenge to change direction. However, rarely does time-governed training provide an opportunity for feedback and accountability. Exams in school provide feedback and opportunity but with little internal growth. "Adult learning" (andragogy) by its design has reflection and accountability built in. With an "Action–Reflection–Action" model, no exams are required. Accountability is provided by the group dynamic. When a student reflects on a past action and dares to try something different next time, internal growth happens. It is the internal growth that makes the disciple. One thing can be said with certainty: the model Jesus used would not fit into a thirty or forty-five-minute Sunday school time slot.

But when one compares the results Jesus got and the growth of His disciples with the outcomes of the Western model used in today's American churches, one must question the effectiveness of the Western model.

I wonder how American Christians would grow and how we would impact our communities if we tried doing discipleship differently. What we have labeled "discipleship" has been relegated to the sacred space we call Sunday school or church. I wonder what discipleship training would look like if we expanded our concept of "sacred space" to include the home and the marketplace. I wonder what discipleship would look like if we moved it from the pedagogy model consigned solely to churches and adopted an andragogy model practiced in our homes, the marketplace, and the church. Remember, Jesus' main thrust in Matthew 28:19 was, "Therefore go and make disciples." This teacher–learner relationship was to happen everywhere these twelve found themselves. By extension, this teacher–learner relationship is to happen everywhere we find ourselves: at home, at work, and at church.

What do we risk? We risk experiencing the powerful effects of God's kingdom invading our homes and communities when we start doing discipleship differently.

Questions for Group Reflection

1. Reflect on your Christian journey to this point. How have you experienced discipleship to this point? How is that similar or different from what you have just read?

2. Here is a nudge toward some honesty. Remember, this is a "no-shame" zone! Is daily Bible reading something you struggle to maintain? Why do you think that is?

3. When you read your Bible, on a scale of 1–10, with 1 being really easy and 10 being really hard, how difficult is it to understand what you read in the Bible? Using the same scale, how difficult is it to hear God speak to you about your everyday life from these ancient writings?

4. When you pray, what kinds of things do you discuss with your Heavenly Father? What would a sample prayer sound like for you?

5. When it comes to connecting with your neighbor, on a scale of 1–10, with 1 being really easy and 10 being really hard, how difficult is it for you to connect with a fellow Christian for the purpose of sharing the successes and struggles of your Christian journey?

6. In Christian circles, we hear a lot about "doing" things for Jesus and His kingdom. These "doing"

activities are often described in terms of being a "fruitful Christian." Focus for a little bit on John 15:5. Does "remain in Me" come before or after "bear much fruit?" Discuss what we might need to change to increase our attachment to Jesus.

Section Two:

Reading Your Bible Devotionally

Why Read the Bible?

Watchman Nee was a Chinese Christian who taught Christian leaders and organized church meetings in China at the beginning of the Communist takeover. He was credited with starting local church gatherings during these difficult times. Nee spent the last twenty years of his life in a Chinese prison, being persecuted for his faith. He died in 1972.

During a Christian workers conference in 1948, Nee made the following observation: "The controversy of the universe is centered on who shall have the authority, and our conflict with Satan is the direct result of our attributing authority to God" (Nee, *Spiritual Authority*).

The question is: why read the Bible? The answer? To bring ourselves more fully under the authority of God. Let me illustrate.

I was sixteen years old and learning to drive. I was taking a class in high school called Driver's Education.

I was dreaming of the day when I would be handed the keys to the family car. Like any teenager, I could not wait to be the master of this fine-tuned, powerful machine!

My day finally came. Dad was getting ready to run an errand. He handed me the keys and said, "I want you to go get the car and bring it around here to the house." This was the day I had been waiting for! I was getting my big chance to get behind the wheel. I wanted to see what this car was made of.

I went to the parking place and unlocked the car. This was going to be easy. I would back the car straight out of the parking place, crank the steering wheel to the left, and back the car uphill onto the pavement. Then I would put it in Drive and follow the street downhill, turn left at the corner and steer the car smartly up to the curb in front of my father. No big deal, right?

Well, my curiosity about the engine size got the better of me. I backed gently out of the parking space, clearing the other cars nicely. I turned the steering wheel to the left to back onto the street pavement. When I felt the rear wheels were off the gravel of the parking space and on the pavement of the street, I punched the accelerator. The rear wheels squealed (to my delight). Then I put the car into Drive and drove the car down the street and around the corner, parking smugly and expertly by the curb in front of my father.

Dad did not miss a beat. I exited from the driver's seat and walked to where he was standing, waiting for me on the sidewalk in front of our house. As I gave him the keys, he asked me a simple question. "Why did you squeal the tires?" I looked down because I did not have an answer. Here he was, a missionary, trying to save every penny he could so we could go back to Africa on time for another term of missionary service. Here I was, a smug teenager who had just shown disrespect for my father's authority. I had also shown disregard for the sacrifices he was making when I shortened the tread-life of the car tires. He was calling my motives into question. It was an important moment for me.

So, here we are at the beginning of this book, talking about studying the Bible. I need to gently ask you a question. Why do you want to study the Bible? Before you answer, we need to take some time here.

Some people study the Bible because they have a task to complete. They are either a pastor, Bible teacher, Sunday school teacher, or Bible student. They may be preparing for a class, a lecture, a seminar, a conference that involves the Bible, or a small-group study. Whatever the case, there is preparation that needs completing. This person is possibly a spiritual leader entrusted with guiding a group toward a better understanding of God's Word. That is a worthy pursuit. I have been there. I can also tell you from experience how dry and unappealing the Bible became when this was the only reason/cause I interacted with God's Word.

Other people study the Bible because they are curious. These people are mostly fact finders. They possibly want to be able to prove somebody else wrong and win a debate or an argument. Others want to know a lot of trivia so that their friends will admire them. They are looking for prestige. I can tell you from experience that this is also a dead-end street. The Bible very quickly becomes a desert, a virtual wasteland. There is no oasis in these wild, arid places. There are no shade trees of Scripture where you can park yourself and rest awhile. There is only the monotony of Bible facts that leave a person's spirit dry and thirsting for Living Water.

Still, others read their Bibles because they believe that is what a Christian is supposed to do. There is not much rhyme, reason, or systematic approach to their reading. These people go to church on Sunday or watch church on TV. For these people, life is a struggle. They did, at one time, start attending church. But for them, church and Jesus were additions to their lives. Their lives are packed with job, kids, and activities. How does anybody find time to do anything else? Do they have time to read the Bible? Hardly. For these people, the Christian life is a roller-coaster experience. There are the spiritual "highs" where a person feels close to God and in love with God. Then there are the spiritual "lows" where a person feels far from God. In these lows, a person sometimes fears being cut off and deserted by God. When a person's foundation is shaking, it is all a person can do to keep their head above water. I know. I have been there too. For these people, Christianity is a performance trap. They feel that if they could do enough for God or His kingdom, God would be pleased with them. If God were pleased with them, they would not feel as if God was distancing Himself. How does a person get out of this struggle? The only way out for me involved full surrender. I had to make God and His kingdom my everything. I found this was the only way to stabilize the ups and downs in my Christian walk. When I committed myself fully to God and His purposes, it was then that I really wanted to read God's Word. I wanted to know what He was saying to me so I could live that out. I find the more I live with God at the center of my life, the better life becomes. The more I engage with God, the greater my joy and the more He speaks to me. This kind of living is indeed a wonderful life!

Then, there is still another group of people. Watchman Nee would recognize these people. These are the people who seek to bring themselves under the authority of God. These are the people whose main desire is to draw close to God. They want their lives under God's authority and dominion. These people are what Jesus would refer to as "kingdom people." These are the people who pray daily, "Your kingdom come, your will be done on earth as it is in heaven" (Matthew 6:10). It is for these people that the Bible becomes a source of life. I am at this place now. What I cannot understand is why it took me so long to get here! This is the best and most satisfying place to be. Since I have been here, I can say from experience that when I go to bed at night, I anticipate with joy the next morning when I will get to spend time with my beloved Creator!

You may be wondering how I got to this stage. Simple. I finally got tired of being at the other places where my spiritual life was thirsty and dry. Nothing satisfied me. It did not matter what I got or acquired in this world. All I truly longed for was the living Breath of God, making me a living soul. All I ever really wanted was the Life of Jesus coursing through my veins. It was when I drew near to God in this way that He drew near to me. Of course, that was His promise all along (James 4:8). That is the place God wants all His children to be (Jeremiah 29:13). And so...God waits.

So, let me encourage you. It is a good thing to examine your motives. Why are you reading your Bible? Where are you in your Christian journey? We are all on a journey to be transformed into the image of Jesus where our worldview looks like His, and our desire to obey the Father resembles the desire He had (Romans 8:29). There is no shame in stumbling. There is no disgrace in falling and getting back up. The only time we lose is if we stop trying. I want to encourage you to take another step. However this day turned out, tomorrow is another day. You can do this. You and Jesus. He will sustain you. Hold His hand and walk with Him. He will strengthen your weak hands and steady your feeble knees (Isaiah 35:3). You do not need to think you are expected to run. All you need to do right now is take Him by the hand. Let Him pour His strength into you. He will cause you to walk again. He will heal you where you are lame. I know. He did it for me.

Questions for Group Reflection

1. Consider the quote by Watchman Nee at the be-
    ginning of this chapter. Now think about what
    you have been taught about or heard about con-
    cerning the lordship of Jesus. How is today's
    teaching similar or different from the quote by
    Watchman Nee?
2. Reflect on your observations of people either af-
    firming or denying God's authority in their lives
    by their behavior. Without naming names, what
    kind of examples come to mind?
3. In your discussions with other Christians about
    why they read the Bible, what reasons seem to
    occur the most frequently? Why do you think
    that might be so?
4. What have you been taught about what it means
    to be a "kingdom person?" How is that similar or
    different from what you read in this chapter?
5. Think about your faith journey to this point. Be-
    fore you answer this question, remember that
    this is a "no shaming/no judgment" meeting.
    What stage do you think you are at? Are you task-
    oriented? Are you a fact finder? Are you reading
    your Bible because somebody told you that is
    what Christians do? Are you really a "kingdom
    person?"
6. How satisfied are you where you are? Why do
    you want to grow deeper in Jesus?

What is the Bible?

What is the Bible? How do people define it? What would someone say about it if you stopped a random person on the sidewalk in a crowded city and asked them the question, "What is the Bible"? You would likely get one of the following answers.

When I asked this question, you probably had an answer come to mind immediately. Those who have been Christians for many years typically think of the answer, "The Bible is the Word of God." In our American culture today, you probably will not hear this answer very much. If you were to then ask a follow-up question, "How do you know this?" this person will possibly respond, "My pastor told us that." They might even reply, "My parents said so," or "That is what my grandparents told me." They might even say something like, "Well, that's what most people say it is." A few people will tell you, "I read the Bible, and that's what I believe it is."

This last segment of people will be few and far between. A Barna Group survey conducted January 15 through February 7, 2019, for the American Bible Society showed the following statistics. Out of every one hundred randomly sampled people in a national survey, the Barna Group found:[1]

- Five would call themselves *"Bible Centered."* They would regularly read their Bible (either every day or several times a week).
- Nineteen would call themselves *"Bible Engaged."* Of this number, only eight would read their Bible every day. Another six would read the Bible several times a week. Two more would read the Bible once a week, and three would read the Bible once a month. The average age represented in this group was forty-nine years.
- Nineteen would call themselves *"Bible Friendly."* Their average age was forty-three years of age. Of this number, about ten attended church in the past week. Another six attended church once in the past six months.
- Nine would call themselves *"Bible Neutral."* Their average age was also forty-three years of age. From two to three of these people have attended church in the last week. Three to four of this number consider themselves unchurched. Three to four of these individuals read their Bibles

once or twice a year. Of this group, two to three will read their Bibles three or four times a year.

- Forty-eight would call themselves *"Bible Disengaged."* Just over half of these people do not consider themselves to be "Christian." Three-fourths of these people will tell you they are unchurched, and almost an equal amount will tell you they never pick up the Bible.

Now you understand why the answer, "The Bible is the Word of God," was not a popular answer in 2019.

Another answer you will probably hear is, "The Bible is God's love letter to us." This answer tends to be a favorite of people new to the Christian faith. This is the answer of someone overcome by the love of God expressed in the sacrificial death of Jesus Christ for humanity. This answer typically applies to only a portion of the Bible, the New Testament. The New Testament is only 260 chapters long, compared to 1,189 chapters in the entire Bible. The New Testament comprises approximately 22 percent of the entire Bible. Why do many young Christians think of the Bible in terms of the New Testament? Because that is where a new Christian usually begins reading. Also, many people new to Christianity begin their readings with the Gospel of John, one of the four Books of the New Testament that focuses exclusively on the life of Jesus.

The Old Testament certainly has a different feel to the Western reader than the New Testament. Like the New Testament, there are several major divisions within the Old Testament. Some seem loving, while others feel cold or harsh.

The Law. This section comprises the primary "instruction" (Hebrew word "Torah") of God to His people. The first five Books of the Bible, Genesis–Deuteronomy, detail how God's people were to live among the nations of the world. To the Western reader, they often come across as inflexible and stern. Not so to the Eastern reader like King David of Israel. Just read what he wrote: "Oh, how I love your law! I meditate on it all day long" (Psalm 119:97).

History. This section contains twelve Books: Joshua, Judges, Ruth, 1 Samuel, 2 Samuel, 1 Kings, 2 Kings, 1 Chronicles, 2 Chronicles, Ezra, Nehemiah, and Esther. The only real love story in this section would be the Book of Ruth. It reads like a romance movie on the Hallmark television channel. While the Book of Esther's main character is the heroine Esther, this Book is a dramatic thriller that will keep you on the edge of your seat. The Books of Ezra and Nehemiah are Books that will mean more to a recovering person. They detail the work involved in rebuilding the spiritual life after captivity (in our modern setting, addiction). The remaining Books read like "true crime" channels on your television channel line-up. There is a lot of killing and bloodshed in the Books of Joshua, Judges, 1 & 2 Samuel, 1 & 2 Kings, and 1 & 2 Chronicles. We need these Books of the Old Testament. They remind us that the spiritual resistance to God's authority and a Christian's Spiritual warfare is a large part of Christian living.

Poetry & Wisdom. In this section, you will find the Books of Job, Psalms, Proverbs, Ecclesiastes, and Song of Songs (also called Song of Solomon). The Book of Song of Songs is the "love" Book in this series. You probably will not hear this Book preached by your pastor. It has a real erotic tone when you read it through. Do not worry! It is safe to read. After all, it is in the Bible and is meant to be read! The Books of Job and Ecclesiastes are recitals of pain that sound like case studies from a therapist's office. Sometimes life hands you one reversal after another. You need to vent to somebody! Proverbs are general wisdom sayings that teach us how to relate to God and our neighbor. Psalms is typically in the middle of your Bible. When you get to the Book of Psalms, you are about halfway through reading your Bible. Psalms is the songbook of the Bible, written mainly by King David. Psalms is a mix of praises and laments. Sometimes you feel like you are up on the mountain top. Other times you feel like you are down in the valley. If I were describing this mixture of praises and laments, I would say that Psalms feels more like the manic/depressive Book of the Bible. Even with this description, if a person is going through a really difficult season of life, Psalms is a great Book to read. It is also great to read when you feel like really bursting with praise to the Lord. There is something about the wording of these Psalms that gets to the real heart of expressing both praise and pain.

Prophetic Books. This section of the Old Testament contains what is called the "major" prophets and the "minor" prophets. These designations have nothing to do with the authors' stature or position in life. These labels have nothing to do with the Books' contents. They refer primarily to the length of the prophetic Book.

- If the Book is long in written length and the focus of the prophetic message is broad, it is considered a "major" prophetic Book (Riggleman, "Who Were the Major and Minor Prophets of the Bible?" 2019). Of these, there are five: Isaiah, Jeremiah, Lamentations, Ezekiel, and Daniel. Of these Books, Isaiah is a Book that feels like a "Bible-within-the-Bible." Isaiah has 66 chapters, and the Bible has 66 total Books. In Isaiah, God shows up near the beginning (Isaiah's vision of

God comes up in Chapter 6). The Bible begins with God in the Book of Genesis. In the last chapter of Isaiah, the prophet concludes with a message of judgment on those who persist in opposing God. The Bible ends with judgment on all those who defy God at the end of the Book of Revelation. Also, Isaiah Chapters 53 and 54 discuss the Lord's "Suffering Servant." The four Gospels of the New Testament (Matthew, Mark, Luke, and John) tell the story of Jesus Christ, God's "Suffering Servant" who was crucified and resurrected for the sins of mankind.

- If the Book is short in written length and the focus of the prophetic message is narrow, it is considered a "minor" prophetic Book (Riggleman, ibid.). Of these, there are twelve: Hosea, Joel, Amos, Obadiah, Jonah, Micah, Nahum, Habakkuk, Zephaniah, Haggai, Zechariah, and Malachi. Although these Books are shorter, they are just as intense as the major prophets.

All the prophetic Books share one singular message. They all sound like a parent who is telling a misbehaving child, "If you keep annoying your brother (or sister), I will put you in time-out!"

A person might see this message as loving from the parent's perspective, but the "time out" session (discussed in the prophets as exile or captivity) from the child's perspective (Israel and Judah) does not feel loving at all. Pain instead of pleasure is on the agenda.

But as you read through these Books, grasping the overall message without getting lost in the details, I think you will discover that God does not give up on His children. They are still part of the family even though they have been chastised, and that is an encouragement to us!

Remember what we said about the answer, "The Bible is the Word of God"? We said earlier that you would get this response probably from only five people out of a hundred. There are many other people who will tell you, "The Bible is filled with wise sayings written by men." This answer is on the other end of the spectrum.

Out of one hundred people, forty-eight to fifty-seven would probably give you the answer that the words of the Bible are of a human, not a divine, origin. What this means is that the people giving you this answer are probably either "Bible Disengaged" (forty-eight) or a combination of both "Bible Disengaged" (forty-eight) and "Bible Neutral" (nine).

Most of the people answering in this fashion most likely see themselves as the final authority governing their lives. They do not intend to come under the authority of the King of the Universe. The apostle Paul speaks to this "authority" power struggle: "The mind governed by the flesh is death, but the mind governed by the Spirit is life and peace. The mind governed by the flesh is hostile to God; it does not submit to God's law, nor can it do so" (Romans 8:6-7).

The outgrowth of this hostility toward God is an inability to understand the things of God. They just do not make sense. The apostle Paul again comments on this: "The person without the Spirit does not accept the things that come from the Spirit of God but considers them foolishness, and cannot understand them because they are discerned only through the Spirit" (1 Corinthians 2:14).

How do you answer a person who is in this position in life? You certainly will not convince them with arguments about all the early documents, translation accuracy over centuries, and best-selling status in bookstores. After all your arguments, they will still see this all as "foolishness" because they are without a spiritual anchor.

Perhaps, the best way to open the door a bit is with empathy. Empathy joins you to another by validating their pain. (This is the same way God worked with us. He sent Jesus to join us in our pain.) Have you ever been lonely, without hope, without purpose for your life, or maybe stuck somehow (as with an addiction)? How did Jesus join you as a friend? How did Jesus believe in you and see great possibility in you? As you gave Jesus authority to redirect your life, how were you led out of a dark place in your life to where you are now? That is your story of redemption! Talk to them to find out what their shattered dreams, broken toys, and wounded lives look like. Then join them in that place with your story. The kind of story that comes alongside another as "friend" and validates their pain and gives them a glimmer of hope is the story that opens the door to Jesus. When they take that step of yielding control of their lives to Jesus, they move into the kingdom of God. They also begin to move in their understanding of what the Bible is from the forty-eight to fifty-seven group, thinking these are the "words of men" to the five who believe it is the "Word of God."

You did not convince them to change their minds. Rather, you helped them open themselves to God so they could have a change of heart. It is the change of heart that makes all the difference!

Questions for Group Reflection

1. Reread the summary of the Barna survey conducted for the American Bible Society in 2019. How shocking was this to you when you read it? Do your experiences and observations confirm or deny the conclusions of this survey? Why do you think that is so?

2. A reading of the lives of the early American Founders appears to support the conclusion that our American republic was founded on scriptural principles. What do you think has contributed to our nation's moral decline and walking away from the Bible?

3. Consider the moral decay of America today. What do you think will be necessary to reverse the spiritual decline of America? Where do you think that will need to start?

4. Compare what you have been taught about sharing your faith with unbelievers. How is that similar or different from the empathy model you read about here?

Plan and Execute

Discipline is central to discipleship. The Book of Proverbs has much to say to that ancient agricultural culture about the benefits of plowing, sowing, and reaping in the right seasons. Proverbs also speaks to the idle person and warns that if he does nothing, he will not eat. This ancient message also speaks to us in our time. If we apply ourselves to the regular reading and study of God's Word, we will nourish our souls. If we do not, we will suffer spiritual malnutrition and stunt our spiritual growth.

As with exercise, it is best to start slowly when creating a habit of daily Bible reading. You see, when it comes to the subject of exercise, athletes are people too. I have never heard of a baby born with toned abs and biceps. A baby is born with all the muscles necessary to become a top athlete. Yet, I have never heard of a baby born into this world an Olympic champion. Athletes take time to train. They begin slow, working up to more exercises and greater strength training.

The journey of athletic training makes a great overlay to formulating a Bible reading plan. Start slow and then work up. I heard of one pastor who was counseling a man who was having trouble with recurring dark thoughts from his past life of sin. The pastor gave this man some good advice. "I want you to read your Bible for thirty minutes a day. Do that for thirty days." At the end of the thirty days, this Christian man came back to his pastor and reported how the light of God's Word was dispelling the darkness. That was wise counsel.

When in conversation with Christians, I have heard them voice on occasion, "I do not know where to begin reading the Bible." This obstacle can seem like a tall mountain that, on the one hand, beckons, but on the other hand, repels. What if you try and then fail? Why not begin where we are, which is on level ground, and then work our way up?

Sometimes, a Bible will have a section in the back of it (close to where the Bible maps are) that is a list of general topics found in the Bible. These are good for short readings. They can range from anything from "Assurance of Salvation" to "Fear" to "Worry" and the like. These are helpful. I used these resources as a young Christian.

Other great resources are smartphone apps. One such app at the time of this writing is the "YouVersion Bible + Prayer App." This app contains Bible reading plans that take a person on an extended reading journey through various topics. Topics include:

- Christian Living
- Wisdom
- Purpose
- Faith
- Trust
- Grace
- Encouragement
- Fasting
- Humility
- Leadership
- Work
- Forgiveness
- Addiction
- New to Faith
- Health
- Suffering
- Finances
- Knowing God
- Missions
- Worship, and various other Christian plans that deal with major church calendar periods.

If a person is going through an extended time of trouble (like divorce or a major life crisis of another kind), there are two places in the Bible to park one's self.

One is the Book of Psalms. You will find this Book near the center of your Bible. The Book of Psalms was written largely by King David of Israel and contains many of his songs of praise as well as prayers of lament. I have personally found great comfort in the Book of Psalms. Another good Book found in the New Testament is the Gospel of Mark. There are times that life gets really crazy. When you feel afraid because you feel like you have no control over your situation, the Gospel of Mark is a good place to read. Mark is the shortest of the four Gospels (16 chapters). One of the distinguishing characteristics I found in a recent reading of the Gospel is how Jesus is shown as a person having control or authority over things everyday people had no control over. Jesus had authority over:

- Demons
- Sin
- Disease
- Waves of the sea
- The Sabbath
- Satan
- Lack of food
- Creation, and
- Death

If you feel like life is out of control, get close to the Person Who has control over everything. I have found that when I get close to the Lord in those times, my spirit calms. As I focus on the Lord of the storm (Mark, chapter 4), the problems I am experiencing become less than overwhelming. That is because I focus on the One Who is the Master of the things that overwhelm me.

Reading sections of the Bible is great when we face tough times. How does a person move from that to a place of having regular interaction with Scripture? It is best if a person new to regular Bible reading begins with a Book of the New Testament. Getting better acquainted with Jesus never goes out of style. For this, I recommend an extended reading of the Gospel of John. The Gospel of John is the only one of the four Gospels that deals with Jesus' supernatural origin in a real plain fashion and does so right from the beginning. John pulls back the curtain and, from the beginning, declares Jesus' divinity and activity in creation. If you are new to the idea of reading through a Book of the Bible, you might try the following Bible reading plan. This plan will guide you in short readings through the Gospel of John over a period of about two months. I have used this plan as a supplement to a ten-week Bible study class. The value of a plan like this is that when a new day comes, you always know where to read because you go to the next unread day and read the section for that day. A plan like this will build a good consistent habit into the daily schedule of your life. Here is the plan.

Table 1 - Reading Through the Gospel of John

Day Number	Date	Bible Reading	Check Finished
1		John 1:1-14	
2		John 1:15-28	
3		John 1:29-42	
4		John 1:43-51	
5		John 2:1-12	
6		John 2:13-25	
7		John 3:1-21	
8		John 3:22-36	
9		John 4:1-14	
10		John 4:15-26	
11		John 4:27-38	
12		John 4:39-54	
13		John 5:1-15	
14		John 5:16-30	
15		John 5:31-47	
16		John 6:1-15	
17		John 6:16-29	
18		John 6:30-40	
19		John 6:41-59	
20		John 6:60-70	
21		John 7:1-14	
22		John 7:15-36	
23		John 7:37-53	
24		John 8:1-11	
25		John 8:12-19	
26		John 8:20-33	
27		John 8:34-47	
28		John 8:48-59	
29		John 9:1-12	
30		John 9:13-34	
31		John 9:35-41	
32		John 10:1-21	
33		John 10:22-42	
34		John 11:1-16	

Table 1 - Reading Through the Gospel of John

Day Number	Date	Bible Reading	Check Finished
35		John 11:17-27	
36		John 11:28-37	
37		John 11:38-57	
38		John 12:1-11	
39		John 12:12-19	
40		John 12:20-36	
41		John 12:37-50	
42		John 13:1-11	
43		John 13:12-30	
44		John 13:31-38	
45		John 14:1-14	
46		John 14:15-31	
47		John 15:1-17	
48		John 15:18-27	
49		John 16:1-15	
50		John 16:16-33	
51		John 17:1-14	
52		John 17:15-26	
53		John 18:1-14	
54		John 18:15-27	
55		John 18:28-40	
56		John 19:1-16	
57		John 19:17-30	
58		John 19:31-42	
59		John 20:1-10	
60		John 20:11-18	
61		John 20:19-31	
62		John 21:1-14	
63		John 21:15-25	

Congratulations! You have completed your first Bible reading plan! Taking a slow start to establish a spiritual habit (discipline) of Bible reading is great.

Compared to the kind of nutrition you're looking for, this first venture is much like the appetizers before the meal. They awaken the taste buds, but your body needs the solid nutrition of a regular meal to thrive. Once a person has a routine down for reading the Bible, the next thing is to move on to the main meal. You might wonder what good, solid spiritual nutrition involves. We can get this nutrition by reading through the Bible in a year. It really is not hard at all. You can find plans online that will help you with that. Personally, I like variety on my reading plate. One daily plan might give you some Old Testament and some New Testament. Another plan might have you reading in a different section of the Bible every day of the week for 52 weeks. For instance:

- Sunday = reading from the *Epistles* (Romans 1-2)
- Monday = reading from the *Law* (Genesis 1-3)
- Tuesday = reading from *History* (Joshua 1-5)
- Wednesday = reading from *Psalms* (Psalms 1-2)
- Thursday = reading from *Poetry* (Job 1-2)
- Friday = reading from *Prophecy* (Isaiah 1-6)
- Saturday = reading from the *Gospels* (Matthew 1-2) (Coley, "Bible Reading")

Another way to read through the Bible is to get yourself a One-Year Bible. This is a Bible that is arranged into 365 daily readings. If you get one for your current year, it will track with the date on the calendar.

Whatever method you choose, the following guidelines will keep you on track and contribute to your spiritual growth:

1. Try to schedule a regular time each day for your Bible reading. Using the same time each day is especially helpful. This time could be every morning, every evening, lunch at work, etc. The main thing is to find a time you can look forward to and stick to.
2. Choose a comfortable place with good lighting.
3. Have paper and pen/pencil handy. Personally, I like to jot references/notes in the margin of my Bible. I have also made notes on verses on an electronic version of the Bible. That way, it is a handy reference the next time I pass that same way. It is like marking your trail when you are hiking. You want to be ready to write because you are expecting God to speak to you. Believe me, He will!

If you have ever been hiking or traveling, you are familiar with what altitude can do for your view. Just climb a mountain and look around. I have often been amazed looking out from the peaks of the Great Smokey Mountains or the Rocky Mountain range. On a clear day, you can see for several miles, and the view is fabulous!

The same holds true for Bible reading. For years I read through the Bible once a year. There came a point when I felt I was getting lost in the details. The terrain was too flat. I really felt I could not see the forest because I was down among the trees! Then I got introduced to reading the Bible through more than one time per year. Typically, if you read three or four chapters a day, you will read through the Bible in a year, 365 days from January through December. The following table will give you an idea of how many chapters per day you will need to read in your Bible to get this mountain-top view.

Table 2 – Mountain-Top Bible Reading

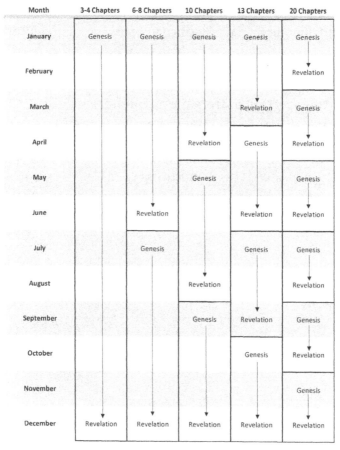

Month	3-4 Chapters	6-8 Chapters	10 Chapters	13 Chapters	20 Chapters
January	Genesis	Genesis	Genesis	Genesis	Genesis
February					Revelation
March				Revelation	Genesis
April			Revelation	Genesis	Revelation
May			Genesis		Genesis
June		Revelation		Revelation	Revelation
July		Genesis		Genesis	Genesis
August			Revelation		Revelation
September			Genesis	Revelation	Genesis
October				Genesis	Revelation
November					Genesis
December	Revelation	Revelation	Revelation	Revelation	Revelation

When you decide to take a more aggressive approach to reading your Bible, you will be amazed at how much of God's plan for the world and for your life you will see. Reading in quantity will give you more Scripture to meditate on. You will be able to remember things that you read earlier in another section of the Bible more easily. The Bible will begin to make a lot more sense to you.

I have found that when I began reading around thirteen chapters a day, God began speaking to me, interpreting Scripture in one place with Scripture from another place. I can tell you from experience that the view is truly spectacular from the mountains.

But you do not get there overnight. It takes steady walking and talking with your Creator. It takes planning, and then it takes executing your plan.

Questions for Group Reflection

1. What is your take on discipline as a central component to discipleship? Now, we must get real honest here. Why do you think our question here either bothers or does not bother you?

2. In what other areas of your life do you use discipline? How does that quality benefit you?

3. If a person applies discipline to their spiritual growth, how do you think that will affect that person's ability to grow deeper in Jesus?

4. To this point in your journey with Jesus, what kind of Bible reading (devotional) plan have you used? Do you feel that has helped or hindered your spiritual growth? What do you think you might try to accelerate your spiritual growth?

5. Read 1 Samuel 3:1-10. In an earlier section, we discussed coming under the authority of God. When it comes to adjusting your Bible reading program, what importance do God's ideas on this subject compare to your ideas on this subject? How do you think God speaks to us today?

6. Compare in your group the various electronic apps you use to help you in Bible reading. What do you find the most helpful? What do you find the least helpful?

7. Talk about reading the Bible through more than one time a year. What kind of impact do you think something like that will have on you growing deeper in Jesus?

What a Difference Culture Makes

Compared to ancient Bible people, modern Americans (and typically Europeans in general) are very mobile. We think nothing of boarding an airplane and traveling to another country where people live differently than we are accustomed to. When we insert ourselves into another culture, it is advisable that we familiarize ourselves with the salient features of that culture. Doing so can keep us from embarrassing ourselves. The same holds true with the world of the Bible. Familiarizing ourselves with cultural differences can keep us from drawing mistaken conclusions from the Biblical text.

When I was growing up in West Africa, we tried to live as "American" as we could in our home. When I stepped out the front door, however, everything changed. The social culture outside our missionary home was vastly different from how we socialized in our home and the United States. As I got older, I was made aware of American accepted norms for getting a wife. American social customs accept courtship preceding marriage. This was not the case in Benin, West Africa. In West Africa, parents arranged the marriages for their children. A prospective groom or father of the groom would approach the father of the prospective bride and arrange the marriage. A "bride price" was always part of the deal. In Benin, the accepted "bride price" (dowery) was two cows and a goat. Courtship that considered the opinions of the prospective bride were never considered. Prospective brides who became Christians, however, spoke out, voicing their refusal to marry a non-Christian man.

With this social environment as my "back-story," imagine my comfort level when I read the Bible story of Abraham sending his servant to arrange for a bride for his son, Isaac. Nobody had to explain that process to me. I was perfectly at ease and comfortable with this social phenomenon that is such a strange story to Americans. Why is it strange? We are worlds removed from the Bible.

Before the Industrial Age, most Americans had agricultural professions. This social construct made Bible stories that emphasize agriculture easy to understand. After the Industrial Age pulled people off rural family farms to city factories, occupations became more specialized. We gradually became less and less familiar with other ways of making a living. We now needed someone to explain the language used by an accountant, an engineer, or a nurse.

When people are so familiar with what everybody does, they need no explanation. This class of people is called a "high context" society by anthropologists. In other words, there is enough generally accepted knowledge of social norms that nobody needs to stop and explain what is going on. By contrast, if the social norms are not generally known to the hearers or readers, this social situation is known as a "low context" environment. I am a "low context" person because I must ask my physician to explain the medical terms used. Without the explanation, I cannot "read between the lines" of the conversation and make an application to my life. The Bible was written for a "high context" audience. We are "low context" readers. If someone does not explain what is going on in the text, we will have a hard time understanding the intended message of our Scriptures so we can make the appropriate application (Malina, Rohrbaugh, *Social-Science Commentary on the Gospel of John*, 16-17). Application is necessary for a lifestyle adjustment. Lifestyle adjustment is what ultimately leads to the transformation into the likeness of Jesus.

The reason for the inclusion of this chapter is to provide a brief overview of these social norms. It is beyond the scope of this book to speak extensively on this subject. It is my hope that the reader will pick up on these strange ways of living and being and will, in turn, begin understanding more of the message of the Bible. It is also my hope that this material will promote curiosity, the kind of curiosity that invites the reader to pursue additional reading on the subject from these referenced authors and others on this subject.

I can guarantee one thing, however. If the reader of this book simply places our modern Western ways of being and socializing as an overlay over Scripture, there is a high probability that this reader will come away from reading Scripture with a message other than what was intended by the scriptural author. That person will fail to hear all that God wishes to convey through His Word.

You may have an objection at this point. "You have traveled to other parts of the world. You have an advantage when you read the Bible. What about me? I have not been out of my state." It is possible to travel without leaving home. Many Americans do this through television programing geared to highlight states or countries. I personally enjoy cooking shows that focus on the foods for which a city or country are famous.

This kind of armchair traveling is what happens when we learn about Bible social customs, the strange ways of being and relating that are unique to ancient Middle Eastern people. When we understand where

Bible people were coming from, Scriptures make more sense. The words we read in the Bible from that cultural "stew" develop a "flavor profile" that can often be quite exciting or revealing.

After my wife and I made our home in Texas, I began traveling to the Middle East without leaving the house. I began reading about Bible culture. One of the first books I picked up was a book entitled *Misreading Scripture With Western Eyes: Removing Cultural Blinders to Better Understand the Bible.* (Richards, O'Brien, 2012).

I also read *The New Testament in Cross-Cultural Perspective* by Richard L. Rohrbaugh (Rohrbaugh, 2006). These books helped me make sense of the culture so that I could, in turn, grab usable meaning from the Bible words I read. If I can better understand how Bible people socialize, then I can more clearly understand how God wants me to relate to others around me.

Those two books were the beginning of my "search for adventure," which continues to this day. Now, climb aboard for a brief visit to the land of the Bible!

Before we embark on our adventure, it will be helpful to have some understanding of the worldview of Bible people. A "worldview" forms the basic lens that brings life into focus. I would characterize their lens, the glasses they looked through, as a pair of bifocals. In other words, we need to consider two basic filters.

First, we have the filter of Time. These people were ancient people. They were not modern people. In our modern culture, we interpret life through the advances of science. We understand that the world is round. We know that the earth rotates on its axis and revolves around the sun. We also know that our sun is a star and that our moon revolves around our earth and that the moon affects the tides of the ocean. How do we know all these things? Science...and telescopes. The ancient people of the Bible had neither science nor telescopes (Walton, *Ancient Near Eastern Thought and the Old Testament: Introducing the Conceptual World of the Hebrew Bible*, 165–167). Considering this perspective of time, we must also understand how little knowledge ancient people had available in their lifetimes. One source quoted Google CEO Eric Schmidt in 2010 as saying, "Every two days we create as much information as we did from the dawn of civilization up until 2003" (Siegler, techcrunch. com, 2010). When we understand this statistic, we can safely assume that the cultural principles we discuss in this section will be relatively stable over the span of time, covering the Old Testament and the New Testament. In other words, the way people socialized and related to each other in the Old Testament is generally the same way they socialized and related to each other in the New Testament. They were all ancient Middle Easterners.

Second, there is the philosophical filter of *Logic*. Logic expresses thoughts and organizes concepts in a meaningful pattern. Our Western civilization has been greatly influenced by the Greeks. Greek logic, expressing primarily the human point of view, was a tightly constructed string of arguments. These arguments proceeded progressively from premise to conclusion (Wilson, *Our Father Abraham*, 150). This logical thought progression we have inherited from the Greeks is called *step logic*. The theology books I have read and the major doctrinal positions (for example, Calvinism and Arminianism) I have encountered are structured using Greek step logic.

The concepts expressed by the Jewish writers of the Bible were different. These "concepts were expressed in self-contained units or blocks of thought" we call *block logic* (Wilson, ibid.). The writers of the Bible felt no need for any "logical" reasoning that arranged these blocks of thought progressively from premise to conclusion. You could have two seemingly unrelated concepts close to each other that appeared contradictory, and they could both be true. One example of block logic might be expressed in Exodus 8:15 and Exodus 7:3. The Bible says that God hardened Pharaoh's heart. The Bible also says that Pharaoh hardened his own heart. Which is correct? Both statements are correct. One is from God's point of view, and the other is from Man's point of view. Understanding the difference between these ways of expressing ideas can make the Bible easier to understand.

Bible people also have a different social structure than Americans. They relate differently with their neighbors than Americans. They also have a self-awareness that is vastly different than we encounter in our Western American culture.

While my parents were on foreign soil in West Africa, one of my father's responsibilities was constructing missionary houses, church buildings in new areas, and Bible School buildings for training pastors. Village churches were built without missionary supervision. Missionary housing and Bible School buildings were another matter.

My father was always the general contractor of the project. He planned the building layouts, arranged for building supplies, and supervised the paid African carpenters and masons. On more than one occasion, he ran out of cement or cinder block. He needed to get more of these building materials from the supplier in the nearest town. As was his custom, he assigned the laborers their duties before leaving the building site. Upon his return with the building materials, he would sometimes find the laborers working. He also sometimes found them sitting in a circle talking. Spending time talking was frustrating to this Western missionary when everybody knew these paid employees needed to be working. There was a deadline to be met. Bricks needed laying on the foundation, and the roof needed completion before the monsoon rains began.

What was the problem? Were these people lazy? This sort of behavior would not be tolerated in the United States! The problem was that the missionary expected the Africans to function like people in America—individualists. These Africans were not individualists. They were collectivists. How does a group of men resolve family or village problems? They sit down and discuss the problem as a collective group until a consensus is reached. There can be no losers in this process. There can only be winners. So, the discussion takes time. The most important thing for a collectivist is group harmony, not a monsoon deadline. There is always tomorrow! When we read the pages of the Bible, we encounter this same cultural conflict.

John J. Pilch, in his book *A Cultural Handbook to the Bible*, discusses the two following terms in detail. The big thing to keep in mind when reading about these Bible people is their approach to life and relationships. The Western (American) worldview is an individualistic worldview. The needs and wants of the individual are primary, while the needs and wants of a particular group(s) to which that individual belongs are secondary.

The Middle Eastern (Bible) worldview is a collectivist worldview (Pilch, *A Cultural Handbook to the Bible*, 78–

83). The needs and wants of the group are primary. The individual serves the group, and so is secondary. Thus, the individual does not choose the group; the group chooses the individual. I have summarized Pilch's narrative into five salient points in the table below.

Table 3 – Collectivist Versus Individualist

BIBLE CULTURE	AMERICAN CULTURE
1. Focus on the group (community) = "Collective"	1. Focus on the individual (self) = "Individualistic"
2. Has an external focus for values & thinking	2. Has an internal focus for values & thinking
3. Willing to adopt group opinions regarding status (honor & shame) and function (trade or job)	3. Forms one's own opinion on a range of issues. Expected to have "self-esteem" and decide individually about function (trade or job)
4. Little mobility in marriage choices, career choices and family living arrangements	4. Great mobility in marriage choices, career choices and family living arrangements
5. Group is strong / Individual is weak	5. Individual is strong / Group is weak

Americans are largely "indoor" and "internal" people. When an American reads key words, the default interpretation is that these words reflect an internal state of being. In other words, an American can "feel" something internally without acting out that feeling.

The opposite holds true for Bible people. In fact, the African society I observed mirrored how people lived in the Bible. Africans I observed, and Bible people I read about were largely "outdoor" and "external" people. Housing was used merely for shelter from bad weather and sleeping at night. In Africa, parts of the house also served as a shelter at night for a few goats, keeping them safe from lions, hyenas, and wild dogs.

When we as Americans read key words in the Bible, we need to step out of our individualist way of thinking. We need to step into the flowing robes of the Middle Eastern person and apply the appropriate external and behavioral extensions. A Middle Eastern person cannot simply feel something without acting on that feeling.

Here is a breakdown of some "trigger" Bible words that give Americans interpretation trouble when they stop at the thinking or feeling level:

Hear. First, the ears hear what is said. However, true hearing can only be considered occurring/complete when the person responds with obedience to what was heard (Tverberg, *Listening to the Language of the Bible*, 3). See Deuteronomy 6:4.

Know. There is more to this than accumulating information. When your world involves a community, one does not fully know until one has had experience or is in relationship (Tverberg, ibid., 5). See Genesis 4:1.

Love. We think of this as a strong positive feeling. A community of people will regard this word as a synonym for the word "attach." The bond of attachment signals the presence of love (Malina, *Handbook of Biblical Social Values*, "Love"). Read John 3:16 again using this understanding.

Hate. Hate is love's opposite pole. If love translates to attachment, it necessarily follows that hate is present when one person detaches themselves either from another person or from a behavior (Malina, ibid.). Read again 1 John 2:9 with this understanding. Now compare what you just read with Jesus' words in John 13:35. See also Proverbs 8:13 and Psalm 97:10. These last two Old Testament verses highlight the behavioral component that must be present to validate a person's love for God.

Covet. The word "covet" and the word "envy" both speak to an individualist of the pain felt upon seeing another person's good fortune. To the collectivist, these words together gain their power through "limited good" (discussed later). In a group, all available honor and goods necessary for sustaining life have been distributed. There is no more to be had. When one person in the group observes someone else obtaining more, that just means someone else in the group must do without. This imbalance disrupts the peace. Restoring the group to a place of harmony and peace becomes the overwhelming concern. How is this end achieved? The successful person can be put in their place through ostracism, ridicule, or insult. Additionally, the wealth gained by this one can be redistributed to the needy either voluntarily or by force. If the successful person does not correct themselves, covetousness or envy takes over to right the wrong. Negative behavior is the natural outcome when a person covets or has envy (Neyrey, *He Must Increase*, 249). When you look at Exodus 20:17 after seeing the behavioral component of coveting, it becomes apparent that the word "steal" would be a viable substitute for the word "covet."

Wise. A good understanding of this word comes from reading the parable Jesus told in Matthew 7:24-27. In this parable, two builders build their houses. "Each house looks secure in good weather. But Palestine is known for torrential rains that can turn dry wadis into raging torrents. Only storms reveal the quality of the work of the two builders" (Carson, *The Expositor's Bible Commentary*, 194). Jesus commended the wise builder not because he had greater knowledge (a Western view). He was commended because he anticipated the storm and factored that into construction that would ultimately save him.

Foolish. Likewise, Jesus presented the flip side of the wise man in Matthew 7. This man was foolish only because his construction work (behavior) did not reflect what he knew to be true (good weather does not last). His indifference led to his destruction.

Once we are accustomed to looking for these words, others will surface in our reading. Take, for instance, the word "remember" in Genesis 8:1a. Noah knew he was the object of God's attention when he either felt or saw the wind, mentioned in Genesis 8:1b. God showed that internal emotion through His external behavior that benefited righteous Noah (Genesis 6:9).

How do we apply this understanding to our lives today? When we read how we are to "love God" with everything we have (Deuteronomy 6:5), we must look for ways to behaviorally attach ourselves to Him. What can we do that will increase our time with Him or our desire for Him? When we read that we are to hate sin, we now understand that behaviorally we are to detach ourselves from the things that God is displeased with. How do we figure that out? We keep reading Scripture to understand what God approves and what God rejects.

We will deal with our neighbor in greater detail later. It is important to mention here, however, that many of the things we attach ourselves to in our American culture negatively impact the people closest to us. If God commands us to "love" our neighbor, He is commanding us to find ways to build a relationship with and a community with those around us. That means anything we do that breaks down harmony and communal bonds is displeasing to God. That is a simple way to figure out what modern behaviors God considers "sin."

Another cultural phenomenon common to both West Africa and the Bible was the norm of honor and shame. When my parents went to Dahomey (Benin), French West Africa, they were part of the second wave of missionaries to enter the country. The uncivilized northern part of the country was where my parents were assigned. It was vastly different from the coastal city of Cotonou, which had frequent contact with Europeans. My parents discovered early in their first term of missionary service that there were many villages that had not heard a Gospel presentation. And because they were largely cut off from the outside world, many of these people had never seen a person of European descent. Dad was in his mid-to-late twenties. On one evangelism trek, Dad took with him a national pastor. It was a good thing he did. Had he been by himself, he would not have evangelized the village.

This was one of the villages that had not yet made contact with Europeans. As was the custom, the first people to greet were the chief and his elders. They determined whether you were welcome and could speak to their village. Also customary was for the chief to greet his visitor with the gift of a live chicken. Dad was carrying his Bible in his right hand. When the chief extended the live chicken to my father, Dad began extending his left hand to receive the gift. At this moment, the national pastor stopped him and offered to accept the gift as his emissary. The gift was properly accepted, and the village was attentive to the Gospel message. On the way home, the national pastor explained this honor code. In Africa, the right hand was considered "clean" (acceptable), while the left hand was considered "unclean" (unacceptable). Accepting a gift with the left hand is a great insult. Insults of this magnitude make meaningful dialogue impossible. To dishonor a dignitary is to become his adversary.

Honor (and its counterpart, shame), is the driving force in a collectivist culture, while guilt drives the individualist (Plevnik, *Handbook of Biblical Social Values*, 114). For the Mediterranean male, honor was "a claim to worth that was publicly acknowledged" (Plevnik, ibid.,106). When we talk about shame in America, we typically do not attach the same meaning to that word that many in other parts of the world attach. The exclamation, "You should be ashamed of yourself!" has more to do with internal guilt than external shame. John J. Pilch references Geert Hofstede (*Culture's Consequences: International Differences in Work-Related Values*, 1980) when he says that "the collectivistic personality type is represented among 80 percent of the current population of this planet. This percentage was quite likely much higher in antiquity" (Pilch, *A Cultural Handbook to the Bible*, 79). According to Pilch, there are more people in the world today that are driven by this external honor code than are governed internally by guilt.

When a person is born into a family, clan, and village, that person is said to have an "ascribed honor" (Rohrbaugh, *The New Testament in Cross-Cultural Per-*

spective, 33). Ascribed honor (reputation) is received at birth. It comes with your family name or place of birth. When a woman is wedded to a man, she becomes dis-embedded from the honor of her birth family and be-comes embedded into the honor of her husband and his family (Malina, *Social-Science Commentary on the Synoptic Gospels*, 30).

Why is all this so important? Having "honor" meant that you had value. This value determined what you had access to in terms of career, goods-for-survival, and marriage partners. The more honor a person had, the more value and the more access that person had. If you were a male, the more shame (dishonor/lack of honor) you had, the less value and the less access to goods you had. If your honor was stripped from you (Jesus' being mocked and flogged before the crucifixion), you sud-denly became expendable (deSilva, *Honor, Patronage, Kinship & Purity*, 31). So, your daily life in the commu-nity was focused on either defending your inherited honor or trying to build on the honor you were born with. Your daily conversations reflected this struggle to either gain honor or avoid shame. Depletion of honor could send you to the poor house!

There is one other factor about honor and shame that is worth mentioning here. Bruce Malina discusses hypothetical degrees of shame. These degrees relate to being shamed in a group. To understand this, one must ask the question: "Now that I have lost my honor in this public forum, how difficult will it be to overturn the shame and regain the honor I lost in the eyes of my peers?"

First Degree Shame: the damage cannot be undone. An example of this would be the rape of a virgin or the killing of a neighbor. The only way now to balance the scales and restore group equilibrium is for the kinsman-redeemer to take revenge on the culprit.

Second Degree Shame: severe damage to the group has been inflicted. However, this shame is not irreversible. There is a way out. The person responsible for the wrongdoing can make a behavioral about-face. If this happens, the honor of the victimized group or family can be restored. An example of this dishonor would be, "I let my daughter marry your son. But now you refuse to let my son marry your daughter."

Third Degree Shame: this was the daily conversational tug-of-war that went on between equals. A challenge to honor would be made. That challenge had to be met. If honor were not defended, honor would be lost (the person would receive shame). This exchange was based on a "winner take all" position. Two men would engage each other. Onlookers determined the winner (Malina, *Honor and Shame in Luke-Acts*, 39–40). In this conversational contest, the first side resorting to violence was considered the loser by the onlookers (Malina, *Rohrbaugh, Social-Science Commentary on the Gospel of John*, 148).

Now that we have examined the major points of this Middle Eastern value, let us see how these points compare to our American individualist culture in the following chart.

Table 4 – Honor and Shame in the Bible

DESCRIPTION	BIBLE CULTURE	AMERICAN CULTURE
1. Where do I fit in this world?	My group is the most important thing in life. Any honor I have comes from my group.	I am my own person. I can join or leave groups at any time. I determine my own value.
2. What values shape how I relate to myself or others?	HONOR – Public claim to worth and public acknowledgement of that worth. SHAME – Public denial of the claim to worth.	Since my group does not control my worth, the only thing that can really hold me back is a sense of GUILT.
3. How do these values affect my ability to survive in this world?	A person was born into a family line (ancestry) and village (place). The honor or shame attached to each determined in large part the kind of work this person would be able to do and the achievements this person would be able to accomplish.	Every person is born a "blank slate." Given the right opportunities and motivation, "the sky is the limit" regarding career choice and personal achievement.
4. How does a person relate to their core value in everyday life (DEFENSIVE or OFFENSIVE)?	DEFENSIVE – Any honor must be defended if one is not to lose their place in the eyes of the group or be able to gain additional honor.	OFFENSIVE – You have to go out and get what you want. If you do not compete offensively, you will not have what you need to get by.
5. What is the main threat to a person's survival in society?	DISHONOR (in various degrees) 1st Degree = No hope of regaining lost honor. This calls for "vengeance" [2nd half of 10 Commandments]. 2nd Degree = Serious damage, but the honor damage might be undone. i.e. intrafamily marriage arrangements between sons / daughters. 3rd Degree = everyday conversational "Push-and-Shove" where a person either defended their honor or acquired additional honor. This is evident especially in the Gospels	The lack of personal opportunity or personal ability.

Now that we have a basic understanding of this value of honor and shame, how does it affect our understanding of Scripture when we use this as an overlay to our reading? We will consider one example from the Old Testament and one example from the New Testament.

From the Old Testament, we will consider the rape of Dinah, the daughter of Leah, who was born to Jacob. This account takes place in Genesis 34:1-31. We will first look at some stated facts and then ask some questions based partly on observation as well as Middle Eastern culture. Finally, we will draw some conclusions based on our discussion of honor and shame.

1. *Facts Listed in Scripture*
    a. v. 1: Dinah was the daughter of Leah, born to Jacob.
    b. v. 1: Dinah "went out" to visit other young women who lived in or near the city of Shechem.
    c. v. 2: The son (whose name was Shechem) of Hamor the Hivite, the prince of the land, caught Dinah and laid with her by force (raped her).
    d. v. 4: Shechem asked his father, Hamor, to arrange a marriage between him and Dinah.
    e. v. 5: Jacob heard about this rape of his daughter, and he remained silent.
    f. v. 7: To say that Jacob's sons were angry when they came in from the fields and learned

about what had happened to their sister would be an understatement.

g. v. 15: The sons of Jacob demanded a bride-price of circumcision of every male in the city.

h. v. 25: Simeon and Levi (sons of Leah, born to Jacob [Genesis 29:33-34]) went into the town of Shechem on the third day while all the men were defenseless from circumcision and put every male to the sword. This included Hamor and his son Shechem.

i. vv. 30-31: Jacob is distraught because he feels his sons Simeon and Levi have made him a target for retaliation to the people of the land. Simeon and Levi justify their actions based on the rape of their sister, Dinah.

2. *Observations and Questions Asked of the Scripture*

a. v. 1: Why was Dinah left unchaperoned when she left the tent of her father to visit the young women of Shechem? It was readily accepted that public space (field, market, city gates) was the domain of males while private space (tent, the interior of a house) was the domain of females (deSilva, ibid., 33).

b. v. 2: One can understand why Shechem, son of Hamor, raped Dinah when he found her in his space. The Middle-Easterner is used to expressing swings of strong emotion. These swings mirror nature, where the desert can be blistering hot during the day and icy cold at night. Put a man and woman together unsupervised, and it is almost guaranteed that somebody is going to get pregnant (Pilch, ibid., "Emotion/Demonstration of Feelings," 56–57).

c. v. 5: One can understand why Jacob remained silent about this outrage. It was customary for the father to blame the daughter rather than the culprit for this outrage (Malina, *Social-Science Commentary on the Synoptic Gospels*, 31).

d. v. 7: One can also understand Simeon and Levi's hot anger over this incident. Dinah's dishonor was a first-degree shaming of Dinah. She no longer had her honor of virginity. Once lost, that could never be regained. Simeon and Levi were Dinah's brothers from the same mother and father. Brothers were the ones who avenged this sort of violation (Malina, *Social-Science Commentary on the Synoptic Gospels*, 31).

e. Generally, the intensity and violence of this episode are shocking to an American. Genders can regularly mix in open areas without fear of personal violence. Of course, Americans have laws that help moderate that sort of conduct. Our legal system also dissuades a person from acting as a vigilante.

3. *Conclusions of this Incident*
   a. We cannot overlay this incident with our American ideas of right and wrong behavior. Jacob and his sons were well within their cultural norms of behavior.
   b. God works with people imbedded within their specific culture to bring about His purposes. What were God's purposes with Jacob? Genesis 28:13-14 tells us that God promised Jacob to give him the land, to make his descendants numerous, and to bless all the families of the earth through his seed.
   c. For us today, God promises stability to all who put their confidence in His instructions and mull them over (Psalm 1:1-3). Are you worried that you may have blown it through bad decisions in your life? You are not that powerful! God factors in our bad decisions into His promises to us and His plans for our lives!

Now, from the New Testament, we examine Jesus' interaction with his townspeople recorded in Luke 4:16-30.

1. *Facts Listed in Scripture*
   a. First, it is important to consider the events transpiring before and after this scriptural segment:
      i. Before: Luke records Jesus, filled with the Holy Spirit, resisting the devil in the wilderness and teaching with power in the synagogues in Galilee.
      ii. After: Luke says Jesus went to Capernaum and taught with authority, cast out demons, healed Simon's mother-in-law, and healing the sick who were brought to Him.
   b. v. 16: Jesus went to Nazareth where He had been raised to manhood.
   c. vv. 17-20: Jesus read from the Prophet Isaiah (Isaiah 61:1-2) in the synagogue.
   d. v. 21: Jesus declared that He was the person God had anointed to live out this prophecy.
   e. v. 22: The townspeople responded by calling Jesus "Joseph's son."
   f. vv. 23-27: Jesus responded to them by talking about a non-Jewish widow and a non-Jewish leper.

    g. vv. 28-29: The people in the synagogue re-
sponded to Jesus with a threat of an act of
violence.

    h. v. 30: Jesus passed through their midst and
went on His way.

2. *Observations Regarding This Exchange*

    a. Jesus was known as "Jesus of Nazareth" (Mat-
thew 26:71; Mark 1:24; Luke 4:24). Jesus did
not have a good honor reputation because
Nazareth did not have a good honor reputation (John 1:46).

    b. The word "fulfilled" used here, in Luke 4:21, is
the same Greek word used in Matthew 5:17,
where Jesus said He had not come to destroy
the Law but to fulfill it. It was customary for
men to discuss the Torah among themselves.
If one in the group thought the one quoting
Scripture misunderstood the commandment so as to violate the commandment or
its intent, they accused the quoting person
of "destroying" the Torah. If the person quoting Scripture upheld the Torah's meaning so
as to obey the commandment, these peers
said he was "fulfilling" the commandment
(Bivin, New Light on the Difficult Words of
Jesus, 93–94). In Matthew 5:17, Jesus said He

had come to fulfill the Law. In other words, He told those gathered with Him that He was God's correct interpretation of what God required. Given this context, it is possible that when Jesus said Isaiah's prophecy had been fulfilled, Jesus could have been saying that He was God's extension to meet the human needs Isaiah described.

c. v. 22: "Joseph's son" is the honor challenge posed by the people in the synagogue. They were saying that Jesus was out of place claiming such honor. After all, if "upstart's" honor grew, someone else would lose honor. There was only so much honor to go around.

d. vv. 23-27: Jesus defended His honor claim by stating that God's blessings extended to others outside the Jewish nation.

e. v. 28: The rage response of the people indicates they felt God's blessings were also in limited supply. If those outside Israel benefitted from God's provision and healing, then those inside Israel suffered. Jesus directed these examples to the people of Nazareth. By implication, Jesus told them the people of Nazareth would not receive God's benefits. To be cut out of God's favor was a big blow to their honor!

f. v. 29: They drove Jesus out of the city and at-
tempted to take His life. From the viewpoint
of the first-century ancient reader, the first
to resort to violence lost the honor challenge
(Malina, Rohrbaugh, *Social-Science Commentary on the Gospel of John*, 148).

3. *Conclusions of this Incident*
   a. While we in modern Western America do
   not subscribe to the honor-and-shame code
   prevalent in the Bible, we still stand before
   God. We are each in the place God has placed
   us with an assignment God has given us. The
   question posed to us is simple. Will we seek
   the Lord and be faithful to His calling?
   b. Most of us today are low-profile people. We
   do not have a large platform from which to
   speak of God's amazing grace. We are day laborers and nine-to-five people. We are hus-
   bands and wives, parents, and children. We
   are ordinary people who go to church on Sunday and then work our jobs Monday through
   Friday. We are single parents, busy dads, and
   soccer moms. While we do not have a reputation that would elevate us to prominence,
   we do have access to the goodness of God that
   can heal brokenhearted people and speak of

God's power to release them from captivity.
We are just...regular Jesus people.

c. The comfort or discomfort of other people
does not nullify the goodness and grace of
God. God's blessing to one does not diminish
God's availability to another. God tells us that
if we reach out to Him, He is available. He is
and has...more than enough supply to meet
every need that we have (Isaiah 59:1)!

"Limited good" was another Bible phenomenon we
encountered in Benin, West Africa. The Africans in the
northern part of the country depended on what the land
could produce for survival. The most common form of
transportation was by foot. If a man was particularly
fortunate, he owned a bicycle. When drought destroyed
the crops, the people experienced famine. American
missionaries did not experience "limited good." We
had vehicles we could use to get food for ourselves from
Accra, Ghana. On African roads, it was about a 448-mile
trip that took over 11 hours. This luxury American missionaries had of getting "more" was unthinkable to the
Africans in Northern Benin.

I clearly recall the bags of food we stored at our mission station for distribution one year. The food was
farina supplied by USAID (United States Agency for
International Development). Why was it at our mis-

sion station? If the American government had given the food to the Benin government, it would have never reached the people who needed it most. It would have gone instead to feed the army, the country's president, and maybe filtered down to a few tribal chiefs. The only relief and hope the village people had was through the missionary.

John J. Pilch, in his book *A Cultural Handbook of the Bible*, presents this concept as a Middle Eastern Bible reality (Pilch, *A Cultural Handbook to the Bible*, 234–235). His discussion mirrors and validates my experience in Africa.

For the most part, Bible people lived off the land. They depended on what the land could produce to feed both people and livestock. If there was drought or locusts, you either stayed and suffered or left your residence in search of "greener pastures" (Ruth 1:1-2). One thing was certain: when you ran out, you could not go to the store for more like Americans are accustomed to. The same went for money. If you regularly found you had more "month" left at the end of your "money," you could not look for a better job. You either did the job your group and reputation allowed you to do (Malina, *Social-Science Commentary on the Synoptic Gospels*, 76-77), or you became a beggar on the side of the road. Sometimes, Americans refer to money as a "limited good" when they use the adage, "Money doesn't grow on trees." Americans, however, typically have a way out or a way up in a decent economy. Historically, Western Americans have shown they can experience an increase without taking what they need from their neighbor by stealing. This was not the case for the Middle Eastern person described in the Bible. The only way to get rich was to take what you wanted from somebody else either by theft, fraud (deceit), or force. For farmers, there was only so much agricultural produce (grain) in any given year. Mark 4:8 speaks of seed landing on good soil and yielding "thirty, sixty, and a hundred-fold." Normal yield from farmland on a good year was two-fold to five-fold. If you wanted more, you had to steal it or barter for it. (Malina, ibid., 202–203).

Once one gets a feel for these hard-and-fast boundaries and the limit the land could produce, one needs to factor in what outsiders took from the land. The following Scripture references are some examples I found that illustrate this harsh reality.

A farmer or livestock owner did not have the total claim to what his land could produce. He struggled because the Torah, the Temple, and the Tyrant (King), made claims on his increase. The following are Scripture notations I have found that illustrate our discussion here. Every one of these entities came to take, and here is what they took:

The Torah

- Leviticus 19:9 and Leviticus 23:22 instructed Israel that when they reaped their fields, they were not to reap the corners of their field or gather the gleanings of their harvest. They were to leave these for the poor of the land.

The Temple

- Leviticus 27:30: the "tithe of the land" is "holy to the LORD."
- Leviticus 27:32: the "tithe of the herd or flock" is "holy to the LORD" (belongs to God only/must be separated for God's exclusive use).
- Leviticus 27:31: If anybody wanted to redeem anything that belonged to the Lord (buy it back for personal use), he had to add 1/5 (20 percent) to its value. For instance, if the grain brought for sacrifice would sell for (in American currency) $100 at the market, the cost to redeem it for personal use would be $120.
- Numbers 18:21: this tithe was to compensate the Levites for their service.
- Numbers 18:26: the Levites were to offer a tithe to the Lord from the tithe they had received.
- Deuteronomy 14:22-29: different tithes are discussed. What does this passage mean?

1. Some Bible scholars say this refers to one single tithe used in three separate ways.

2. Many Jews (including Josephus, a famous Jewish historian) believe this describes three separate tithes the Jews were responsible for giving over the period of six years (rather than one tithe used in three ways).

The Tyrant (King)

- 1 Samuel 8:10-18: The king could confiscate the best fields, vineyards, and olive orchards to give to his servants. He could also take one-tenth (the king's "tithe") of the grain and vineyard harvest as well as one-tenth (the king's "tithe") of the increase of flocks or herds for his servants.

Now, imagine yourself, a humble farmer who planted barley this year. You are trusting the Lord God for a good harvest. You are hoping for rain. You want to be faithful to the Lord. So, you do not reap to the corners of the field. You reap the middle area of your field, leaving the corners. Then, after the Temple and the Tyrant come through and take their share, you look at what you have left. You set aside the grain necessary to plant barley again next season. What is finally left is what you have available to feed your family this year! How will you survive without stealing or begging? Now factor in additional taxes imposed by Rome in the New Testament (take note of the reason for the decree by Caesar Augustus in Luke 2:1-3). This is what we mean when we talk about "limited good."

Survival in a peasant culture is another Bible culture reality. In America, individual effort is applauded. Getting something just because you have connections is frowned upon. A person who gets a promotion at work because of a good relationship with the boss quickly finds himself or herself an outsider to the fellow employees they once talked to on breaks. It is not uncommon in the business world to suspect the integrity of the individual who suddenly has a meteoric promotion to a much better position! This attitude toward special treatment is behind the government agency of the SEC and laws that prohibit insider trading. In America, if something is too good to be true, it probably is not true.

West African collectivist culture was structured in a totally different way. If you wanted to get ahead, you really had to know somebody who had connections. During my later teenage years, my parents ministered in the country of Nigeria. Sometimes, governmental business needed to be tended to for the benefit of the missionary work. Often the problem had to do with resident visas. It was not uncommon for the missionary to travel to the nearest government offices, sometimes 30–40 miles away, only to learn that the official in charge of visas that day was "off seat." He either had a family emergency, took a vacation day, or simply did not want to be bothered. "Come back tomorrow" was the typical response. Taking two or more days off from vital missionary work with little hope of success is not an efficient way to conduct God's kingdom business! How could a missionary overcome these obstacles? I can tell you one thing. The missionary will not survive unless he realizes his "American" way of doing business has no exchange value in the African cultural market. Sometimes, you must play the game the way the African plays it. How is that? You put some extra money in his palm to grease the wheels of efficiency. You did not "bribe" him. That is an American cultural understanding. From the African perspective, you helped him so he could help you. In a peasant culture and in a collectivist society, this kind of survival is closely tied to "limited good." What is true in West Africa was also true in the Middle Eastern culture of the Bible. You had to know somebody. You had to have "somebody on the inside."

In biblical culture, you could not survive acting as an individual. Survival required a community, hence, the "collectivist" society. The local market had the small items used for day-to-day needs. What about food if you ran out? What happened if you experienced drought in the land? You needed the help of a powerful person, one who could supply your limited and lacking necessities.

You needed a "patron." David A. deSilva does an excellent job of explaining this reality in his book *Honor, Patronage, Kinship & Purity – Unlocking New Testament Culture* (deSilva, 96–99). The patron would supply you with the goods or services you needed to survive for another year. If you did not have direct access to the patron, you went through a broker who had that kind of access and could appeal on your behalf to the patron. This broker was called a "friend." What did you owe the patron in return? Your loyalty and praise. Your public and prolific praise of the patron would build the patron's honor status in the community. This was a long-term and reciprocal relationship. You got what you needed to survive. In return, the patron received your praise and honor, and often a "tribute" off of any of your increase. He got his cut for his services.

The Old Testament example of this relationship can be found in Genesis 41. Pharaoh is the patron, and Joseph is the broker or friend.

A New Testament mention of this relationship can be found in Luke 7:34 and Matthew 11:19. The Pharisees and experts in the Torah claimed to be close to God because of their strict observance of the Torah commands. When they referred to Jesus as the "friend of publicans and sinners," they were mocking Jesus' claim that He had direct access to God and could get these irreverent Jews' favors from God (forgiveness of sins) that they couldn't get for themselves. This attitude came from the Pharisees' claim that right standing before God came from Torah observance.

I have used the following diagram to illustrate deSilva's comments on this subject.

Table 5 – Clients, Patrons and Friends

A Middle Eastern Model of Relationships

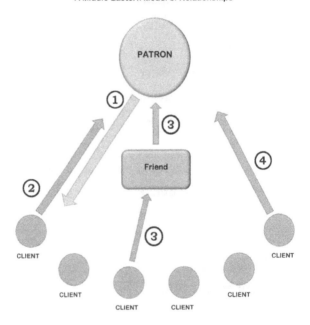

Goods and Services: All goods and services are limited. "More" comes through a "Patron."
Patron: Has access to all the goods and services you will ever need.
Client: Does not have access to enough goods and services to get by and make ends meet.
Friend: Is a "broker" between the Patron (who has the goods) and the Client (who needs the goods).

1. The Patron gives goods (Favor)to the client and supplies needs, which includes providing protection from enemies (part of a covenant).
2. The Client repays the Patron with loyalty and praise.
3. When the Client has a need, he goes through the "Friend" who has access to the Patron.
4. The Client pays a "tribute" to the Patron from material gain for favors rendered and to show that the Client honors the Covenant.

American individualists practice hospitality. Depending on what region of the United States you hail from, the level of hospitality shown increases or decreases according to what section of America you live in. Southern cattle farmers have a reputation for being more open within their communities than Northern big-city dwellers. I know, these "broad-brush" characterizations are illustrational only. I also know these characterizations are based on stereotypical perceptions. I will hasten to point out that a Midwesterner like me is easy to spot in both the North and the South!

When you are living, working, and relating in a group, you know who all the members are. This was especially true in Bible times. Everybody knew their neighbor. Everybody also knew when a stranger came to the town or village. The arrival of strangers was always a big deal. Strangers could represent either opportunity or threat. How will this stranger fit in? Are they safe? What opportunity or threat do they pose to the community? The answers to these questions formed the argument Hamor and his son Shechem presented to the civic rulers at the city gate. This proposal to accept the terms of circumcision was based on the presumption that the strangers (Jacob and his sons) were a safe bet for the community (Genesis 34:20-23).

Strangers had to be checked out because every community of family/friends was a "closed" community. Every newcomer was suspect until cleared. The normal vetting was not done by a detective attached to law enforcement. It was handled by the regular people of the community.

There was a process used to discover whether this outsider should be considered a "friend" or an "enemy." The word describing this vetting process is "hospitality" (Malina, *Handbook of Biblical Social Values*, "Hospitality," 115).

See the table below to find out how this worked in the ancient world.

Table 6 – The Ancient Code of Hospitality

DESCRIPTION	BIBLE CULTURE	AMERICAN CULTURE
1. Object of Hospitality ("Who is hospitality directed toward?")	Strangers ("outsiders" = anybody outside the "in-group" that is deemed "unsafe")	Friends and family ("insiders" = only the "safe" are offered hospitality. The "unsafe" are rejected.
2. Goal of Hospitality	Turn strangers ("out-group" and therefore "unsafe") into friends (accepted part of the "in-group" that is deemed "safe."	No conversion is necessary because only friends and family (the "safe") are offered hospitality.
3. Before Hospitality is offered	The "stranger" is tested to determine if he will fit into the known group ("safe") and not threaten the group	The "stranger" is tested to determine if he / she can be a "friend" to whom hospitality can be offered.
4. Formal point of "conversion" from "stranger" to "friend"	Foot washing is the point where the stranger is converted from "stranger" to "friend"	No formal act that signals conversion from "stranger" to "friend"
5. Responsibilities of "GUEST"	a. Do not dishonor ("shame") the host. If you do, he will become your adversary ("enemy") b. Accept whatever is offered c. Stay in assigned spaces d. Do not assume host's authority e. Praise the host (increase the host's honor) upon leaving.	Similar rules of conduct that generally follow "Rules of Etiquette"
6. Responsibilities of "HOST"	a. Do not dishonor ("shame") the guest. If you do, he will become your adversary ("enemy") b. Offer generously from your provisions c. Protect the guest in your space d. Use authority to protect the guest from hostility e. See the guest off on their journey	Similar rules of conduct that generally follow "Rules of Etiquette"

When viewed through this lens of hospitality, God's welcoming activity to sinners ("outsiders") takes on new meaning as we explore Scriptures from this ancient value. See the table below.

Table 7 – Scripture Through the Lens of Hospitality

SCRIPTURE	HOSPITALITY'S LENS
Ephesians 2:13 ¹³But now in Christ Jesus you who once were far away have been brought near by the blood of Christ.	Salvation is God showing hospitality, thus turning "strangers" into "friends."
John 13:4-5 ⁴ so he got up from the meal, took off his outer clothing, and wrapped a towel around his waist. ⁵ After that, he poured water into a basin and began to wash his disciples' feet, drying them with the towel that was wrapped around him.	The point in time when the disciples went from being "strangers" to God's family to being "friends" in God's family. God is the "Host" with Salvation and assumes the responsibilities of the "Host."
John 14:17 ¹⁷ the Spirit of truth. The world cannot accept him, because it neither sees him nor knows him. But you know him, for he lives with you and will be in you.	The Believer becomes the "Host" to the Holy Spirit and is then liable for the responsibilities of a "Host" toward the Holy Spirit. The Holy Spirit is the "Friend."
Ephesians 4:30 ³⁰ And do not grieve the Holy Spirit of God, with whom you were sealed for the day of redemption.	Do not shame your "Friend." If you do, He will become your adversary ("enemy").

Nothing brought families together better than a wedding. In the Middle East, as in most parts of the world, a wedding is cause for a great celebration. This is the reason why a reading of John 2:1-11 brings a sense of joy at the point of reading this gospel account. Typically, a matchmaker was involved in the process. This was too important an event to be left to chance! The life and tranquility of the community were at stake! How could the prospective groom and bride be expected to understand personality differences and family types?

They could not! Unthinkable! So, a matchmaker was a necessity.

The groom could potentially acquire additional honor by marrying a virtuous woman (Proverbs 31:1-31). Even though this last chapter of Proverbs extols his wife, it is the husband who is really "crowing" about his increase of honor!

The bride could potentially either maintain ascribed honor (her family's standing and value in the community) or destroy it by stepping out from under her father's authority and becoming pregnant outside of marriage. Her father's honor was maintained in the community if he succeeded in keeping his daughter undefiled until she went to her husband's house. If he were not successful, his honor was lost and could not be regained. We read from the prophet Isaiah in Isaiah 53:3, "He was despised and rejected by mankind, a man of suffering, and familiar with pain. Like one from whom people hide their faces he was despised, and we held him in low esteem."

We tend to think the timing of this was closer to the crucifixion. It was not. The application of shame was before His birth because the gospel writer Matthew records in Matthew 1:18, "This is how the birth of Jesus the Messiah came about: His mother Mary was pledged to be married to Joseph, but before they came together, she was found to be pregnant through the Holy Spirit."

The event we celebrate each December brought shame and pain on both Joseph's and Mary's families.

The birth of Jesus was at the same time unusual, tragic, and miraculous. Being in the center of God's will does not always lead to joy and peace. Sometimes it brings pain and suffering. This was the story of Jesus from the moment of His conception through His death by crucifixion.

Thankfully, the story of Jesus was not the norm for the average Bible person. Because most marriages were joyful and honorable events, the apostle John could refer to Christians as the Bride of Christ. He records in Revelation 19:7, "Let us rejoice and be glad and give him glory! For the wedding of the Lamb has come, and his bride has made herself ready."

The following table describes the marriage ritual of the ancient world. It also ties many Scriptures in the New Testament to this subject. Much of the information in this chart was gleaned from a Jewish Seder explanation at Capstone Church, Benbrook, Texas, April 2019.[2]

Table 8 – The Bridal Sequence in Scripture

PROCESS	SCRIPTURE
1. **Proposal** – After the matchmaker finds two prospective persons, it is up to the prospective groom to propose to the prospective bride. At a festive occasion at her father's house, he gives her a cup of wine. If she accepts and drinks the wine (the symbol of a blood covenant) she accepts his proposal of marriage.	**Matthew 26:27-28** [27]Then he took a cup, and when he had given thanks, he gave it to them, saying, "Drink from it, all of you. [28]This is my blood of the covenant, which is poured out for many for the forgiveness of sins. **NOTE:** John 13:26-30 has Judas receiving the sop at the beginning of the meal and leaving the group before the Last Supper (bread & wine).
2. **Betrothal** – a formal act of property transfer where the groom gave his bride one dinar (one silver denarius, the value which was about 20 cents and was the daily wage of a soldier or a day laborer). The husband then told the bride that through it (the dinar) she became betrothed to him 'according to the law of Moses and Israel'.	**1 Peter 1:18-19** [18]For you know that it was not with perishable things such as silver or gold that you were redeemed from the empty way of life handed down to you from your ancestors, [19]but with the precious blood of Christ, a lamb without blemish or defect.
3. **Separation – GROOM** – Groom goes back to his father's house to prepare a living quarters for him and his bride. When the father says the house is finished, he sends the groom to collect the bride.	**John 14:2-3** [2]My Father's house has many rooms; if that were not so, would I have told you that I am going there to prepare a place for you? [3]And if I go and prepare a place for you, I will come back and take you to be with me that you also may be where I am.
4. **Separation – BRIDE** – Bride is given about twelve months to provide for herself. The bride prepared her clothes and adornments.	**Ephesians 5:25-27** [25]Husbands, love your wives, just as Christ loved the church and gave himself up for her [26]to make her holy, cleansing her by the washing with water through the word, [27]and to present her to himself as a radiant church, without stain or wrinkle or any other blemish, but holy and blameless. **Revelation 7:9** [9]After this I looked, and there before me was a great multitude that no one could count, from every nation, tribe, people and language, standing before the throne and before the Lamb. They were wearing white robes and were holding palm branches in their hands.
5. **Going to the Groom's House** – The bride goes with great fanfare and procession to the house of the groom. The groom goes out to receive her into his house.	**1 Thessalonians 4:16-17** [16]For the Lord himself will come down from heaven, with a loud command, with the voice of the archangel and with the trumpet call of God, and the dead in Christ will rise first. [17]After that, we who are still alive and are left will be caught up together with them in the clouds to meet the Lord in the air. And so we will be with the Lord forever.
6. **The Wedding Ceremony** – was essentially the groom's introduction of the bride into his	**Revelation 19:6-9** [6]Then I heard what sounded like a great

father's house. An important part of this celebration was the feast. The entire celebration lasted seven days.

multitude, like the roar of rushing waters and like loud peals of thunder, shouting: "Hallelujah! For our Lord God Almighty reigns. [7] Let us rejoice and be glad and give him glory! For the wedding of the Lamb has come, and his bride has made herself ready. [8] Fine linen, bright and clean, was given her to wear." (Fine linen stands for the righteous acts of God's holy people.) [9] Then the angel said to me, "Write this: Blessed are those who are invited to the wedding supper of the Lamb!" And he added, "These are the true words of God."

Mark 14:23-25

[23] Then he took a cup, and when he had given thanks, he gave it to them, and they all drank from it.

[24] "This is my blood of the covenant, which is poured out for many," he said to them. [25] "Truly I tell you, I will not drink again from the fruit of the vine until that day when I drink it new in the kingdom of God."

I began this section by making mention of the wedding traditions of West Africa. I did mention the practice of giving and receiving a dowery. What I did not mention was that in West Africa, as was practiced in the Middle East, the bride typically stayed in the house of her father until marriage. When it was time for her to be given in marriage, the groom went to the bride's father's house. He then took his bride with him to his father's house, where she became part of a new family group.

These African customs were similar in many ways to the culture of the Bible. Honor codes were also similar. What I have referenced in this section is but a small sampling available when one studies the Bible from the perspective of the social sciences. More examples, while tantalizing, are beyond the scope of this book.

I do hope the examples presented here prove foundational. I trust they prove useful in building a bridge between the ancient Bible culture and where we live today. If we walk on that bridge, we will grow in Holiness—a people set apart by God and for God and His kingdom.

I think you can see at this point that God is readily active in His world. Because He is active and engaged, we experience Him at different times in various locations. Let me ask you a question. How and when do you experience God? You might want to think about this a bit because it will most likely affect how you encounter your day. Let me tell you about my first up-close experience with God.

I was not yet ten years old. Our family was in West Africa at our second missionary station. My father was planning a trip to another West African country, Ghana, where we could stock up on canned food. We did this about twice a year. Since a trip like this was rare, it was a real treat for me! I went outside to check on my father. He was feverishly working on a flat tire for our vehicle. I asked him what he was doing. He told me that the tire was flat and that he was having trouble getting it to hold air. This was one of the "new" tubeless tires! It was new to me as I had only experienced tubed tires to that point. If you got a flat, you removed the tube from inside the tire, patched the tube, and then put it back inside the tire between the loose tire and the rim. When the tube was filled with air, the edge of the tire made contact with the rim. You had a good tire again! Easy, right? My dad said this was not that way. On a tubeless tire, you had to get the edge of the tire that touched the rim to "seat." There had to be a solid connection of this part of the tire to the rim, or the air would leak out as fast as you filled the tire with air. He was having trouble getting this tubeless tire to "seat" properly on the rim and so it would not hold air. He then told me that if he were not successful in his efforts, the trip would be canceled.

I turned away and went back into the house. I was so afraid of missing out on an adventure I had been counting on. I remember praying and asking God to help my father find a way to get the tire fixed. A while later, Dad came into the house and announced success. I was overjoyed! I asked him what he had done. Dad had steel banding and a banding tool used to stabilize wooden crates. In those days, missionaries crated large belongings for shipment between the United States and Africa. Suitcases were for clothes only. Everything else went by ship across the Atlantic. A wooden crate reinforced externally with tightened steel banding typically kept everything safe and orderly until it reached the other continent.

How did my dad fix the tire? He took a length of steel banding and wrapped it around the circumference of the tire in the middle of the tread. He then took a banding tool and tightened the strap down. This central pressure forced the bead edge of the tire firmly against the rim. At this point, my dad began filling the tire with air. When the internal air pressure was enough to hold the bead of the tire securely against the rim, he released the steel banding. He could now fill the tire up to recommended pressure.

This meant our trip was on. We were going to Ghana, and I was elated! I also recognized at that moment that this was the first time I could remember God hearing and answering my prayer. It was my prayer that I prayed. I am sure my dad was praying too. But it sure felt like God was smiling at me with a face full of love and delight! I remember this as the first time after my conversion that God heard and answered my prayer.

As I continued growing and maturing, there were other points along the way where God seemed to interrupt the course of events in an ordinary day. Looking back at my life from my current vantage point, I recognize a belief that grew over time. This belief was that God, on occasion, will interrupt your life in a dramatic fashion. It is this "Ta-Dah!" entrance of His that we called answered prayer. If God made a really grand entrance that was a real showstopper, we called that answer a miracle. It had no other explanation. But where was God the rest of the time? He seemed to be usually silent and generally absent, except for those times that He proved to be a welcomed interruption at a critical time.

This belief about prayer certainly affected my prayer life as I got older. I did not have a prayer life unless there was something I really needed or wanted. God did not seem to be interested because He never seemed to show up on a regular basis. At worst, He seemed like an absentee father, and at best—a long-distance father. As an absentee, God was busy with His own stuff and rarely thought of me. As He was a long-distance Father, I was on His mind, but He rarely showed up. This erroneous belief had a marked influence on my Christian growth and maturity. My Christian life was plagued for years with missteps and pitfalls and a constant swing of emotional ups and downs. I was anything but secure or stable.

Now, does any of this sound familiar to you, or am I the only one? I have a feeling that you may have grown up, too, with this understanding of an absentee God. Many people do. This is one view that permeates the aquifer of our American educational system. We are taught in school that, at best, God rarely gets involved in everyday life. Generally, God started this universe and then backed away to let it do its own thing. Every-

thing runs fine by natural laws without God's intervention. This generally appears to be the definition of the
word "Deism" (Merriam-Webster.com). It is this view
that is presented in our schools as the predominant religious view of many of the founders of this Republic
we call America (Kidd, "What 'Deist' Meant to Thomas
Jefferson," 2020).

When we see God as mostly silent and largely absent from daily life, our spiritual lives feel sluggish and
anemic. What is the cure? I believe the cure must come
through a paradigm reset. Such a reset is offered in a
quote by Old Testament Professor John Walton. He
states the following: "It would be difficult to discuss
with the ancients the concept of divine intervention,
because in their worldview deity was too integrated
into the cosmos to intervene in it" (Walton, *Ancient Near
Eastern Thought and the Old Testament*, 87).

How did ancient Bible people experience God? It
certainly was not the way I just described in the account of my growth to maturity. For the ancients, God
was totally integrated into the world. This was true for
the nations of the world as well as God's chosen people,
Israel.

Most of the evidence we have today about how the
ancient nations thought about their gods comes from
the writings preserved from Babylonia and Assyria.
These were the two pagan nations God used to take His
people out of the Holy Land because of their unfaithful-
ness (Habakkuk 1:6,12; Isaiah 7:17-25; Isaiah 1:1-9).

Professor Walton provides an ancient overview. The gods of the nations, according to ancient writings, appeared as an elevation of the human family. There were males and females that had offspring. In their relationships, they experienced jealousy, anger, and hatred. In their work, they controlled weather elements that were instrumental in making food grow. The gods had humans serve them. Life for humans could get chaotic because the gods often vied for power and preeminence among themselves. They appeared as a reflection of humanity. Humans communicated with the unseen gods through visible idol images (Walton, ibid., 102–105, 114–116).

The God of Israel was a different story altogether. The first four of the Ten Commandments, as seen in Exodus 20:1-11, provide the contrast. Again, John Walton gives us an ancient perspective.

1. Exodus 20:1-3, "no other gods": God tells Israel that, unlike the surrounding nations, He works alone. The God of Israel has no "wife." He needs no help...period. Since God has all authority, the gods of the nations have no standing in God's presence (Walton, ibid., 155-160).

2. Exodus 20:4-6, "no image": The God of Israel does not communicate at a distance through an image. He can be personally known.

3. Exodus 20:7, "not misuse the name of the LORD your God": God's name is tied to His purpose. When a human pursues his own purposes using a cover of God's name, he is taking the name of God in vain. In today's world, we call this "identity theft" (Walton's words).

4. Exodus 20:8-11, "remember the Sabbath": This positive commandment at the conclusion of three negatives harkens back to Genesis 2:1-3. The Genesis account of the Sabbath is a picture of the God of the universe becoming fully engaged with His ordered Cosmos. He assumes His place of authority when He "rests" on His throne (Walton, "Interpreting the Creation Story," 2015).

When I began seeing God through ancient eyes, I started getting a fuller picture of an awesome God who is vitally present. He is not far away. Though unseen by human eyes, God is significantly involved in the world that He made to be my home.

Now, looking back on my childhood, I no longer imagine an absentee or long-distance God. Now, prayer has become so much more than a set time once a day or once a week. Prayer, for me, has become an ongoing conversation with the God who loves me, cares for me, and provides for me. So, I must ask, how about you?

Questions for Group Reflection

1. Reflect on what you just read about ancient and Middle Eastern culture. What surprised you the most? What surprised you the least?

2. Compare the ancient worldview to our modern worldview. Discuss how this might shift our understanding of the Creation, recounted in Genesis 1-2. How has this shifted your understanding of the authority of God in our universe? What effect might this have on a Christian's ever-increasing faith and attitude toward prayer?

3. Read Luke 7:34 and Matthew 11:19. Now revisit the chart called "A Middle Eastern Model of Relationships." Many American Christians think that if they can either do more or be a better Christian, they will increase in favor with God. What effect does this Middle Eastern concept have on what we know as "Performance Christianity?"

4. Read 1 Corinthians 6:19. Compare that to the section describing the hospitality code. Discuss how you understand this verse when you see it through the lens of hospitality.

5. Compare the ancient understanding of God's integration in this world with the modern understanding of God's absence from this world. How

do you think this ancient understanding might deepen your prayer life?

6. Read Exodus 20:7. What have you heard taught about what it means to take God's name in vain? How does that compare with the ancient understanding?

7. When it comes to "taking God's name in vain," in what kinds of ways do you see "identity theft" of God taking place in modern American Christianity? What might this have to do with the concept of the authority of God?

Your Culture Versus God's Authority

Everybody has likes and dislikes. Just ask a child, "What is your favorite color?" They will tell you. They might know what they like, and then, they might not. Trying to please the adult asking the question, a child might answer based on what he/she thinks the adult wants to hear.

Ask an older person, "What is your favorite color?" This person now has many years of life experience behind them. By now, this person knows which colors make them feel happy, peaceful, or good about themselves. At this stage in life, there are some colors that either put a smile on the face or a smile in the heart. An older person will probably tell you the color that makes them feel the best.

Compared to the child who wants to please the adult, the older person will tell you what he/she really likes. This person has a preference.

In an age when authority is either questioned or blatantly ignored, one of the first realities to face the gallows is Truth. Question a younger person's life choices with an appeal to the authority of Truth. What you will probably hear is the answer, "Well, that may be true for you, but it is not necessarily true for me." What has this young person done by answering this way? They have just defined "truth" as synonymous with "preference." When you come to the fork in the road, there is nothing that gives stability. There is no moral compass, no "True North." Everything is left now to preference. When important life decisions that have long-term consequences are based on "preference," you have just reduced life to asking the question, "What is your favorite color?" The important life decision is just...not important. Now question how they will feel about life five, ten, or twenty years from now. They cannot answer that. They just know how they feel now, and that is all that matters.

Traveling using a GPS device speaks to deciding between truth and preference. It is much easier than it used to be when a fold-up map was the only option. I grew up in the age of paper fold-up maps. It was the age before personal computers. GPS? What was that?

In the days before the interstate highway system, you got from point "A" to point "B" either by memory or by using a highway map. If you were traveling alone, memory was your best ally. But what about a greater distance? What if you wanted to travel by car from New York to Los Angeles? A journey of great distance was easier with a traveling companion.

There you were, driving along, keeping your eyes on the road. Beside you in the front seat was your companion, a "navigator" as it were, with a foldable map spread out on the lap. "Take this highway until you get to highway thirty-five. Then turn left." "Uh-oh! I think you just missed your turn!"

Gone, now, are the days of the foldable paper maps from the gas station. Now we use a small electronic device that communicates with a satellite global positioning system (GPS). We no longer hear, "Uh-oh! I think you just missed your turn!" We now hear "Recalculating" or "Make a U-turn!" Now, as you are driving, if you decide you know better than your GPS, be prepared for digital confrontation. If your GPS does not recalculate, it will continue harassing you to turn around until you are ready to throw it out the window!

How do you take care of this problem between your preference and your GPS device's preference? All maps, whether paper or electronic, operate on the same principle. A starting location is required if you want to calculate the best route to your destination. How do you fix that pesky GPS device? It may require a reboot. You might have to disengage its life source. When you reconnect it to power, it is going to ask you for permission to use your location. When you answer in the affirmative, it will then calculate the best route to your destination. Now you are free to roam about the country.

You may ask, "What does traveling have to do with truth and preferences?" There are people today who feel there are many roads to heaven. They say, "Jesus is not the only way. After all, there is 'your truth,' and then there is 'my truth.'" How can a person be sure that one person's claim has more authority than another person's claim? Eugene Peterson, author of the Bible paraphrase, The Message, put it this way. "If we don't know where we are going, any road will get us there" (Peterson, 2005, 1).[3] The destination you reach will largely be determined by what you choose as your navigation aid.

In American culture, people typically live their lives according to culture or according to preference. "Everybody else is doing it!" Who wants to be the only person doing something different? Now that's peer pressure! Who wants to have everyone else talking behind your back or cracking jokes about you? Don't you want acceptance?

Who wants to be passed on the highway with people giving you those long, angry looks? After all, everybody is exceeding the speed limit. Who wants to come to a complete stop at the stop sign? After all, the guy behind is surely in a hurry, and you will get the horn (or worse).

When you are trying to do what is right, and everybody else is pressuring you to just go along, that is a sure sign that Culture is in the driver's seat. There used to be a bumper sticker years ago that read, "Jesus is my co-pilot." It did not take long for someone to produce a second bumper sticker as an answer to the first. The second one read, "If Jesus is your co-pilot, you're sitting in the wrong seat."

Can I say this? If Culture rather than Christ is calling the plays of your living and directing your behavior, you are listening to the wrong navigation aid. How does a person get rid of the annoying cultural voice that demands compliance? To get rid of that annoying voice on your GPS device that demands a U-turn, you need a reboot. You need to turn the guidance system off and make a fresh start.

In life, everybody needs a reboot. Instead of getting a reset to a satellite, a person needs to be reset to God. How does that happen? Every person needs to die. What? No, not literally! Spiritually! When a person comes to God and accepts God's substitute, Jesus, as the final remedy for man's rebellion, a trade takes place. God accepts Christ's death in the place of our own. What happens next is really something beyond description. Enough to say that when God accepts Christ's death instead of our own, then God gives us the spiritual life that belonged (rather belongs) to Christ. You see, Jesus literally died for the sins of mankind. But God would not let Jesus stay dead. God raised Jesus from death physically. Because of the resurrection of Christ, we can get plugged into a new power source. We get spiritual life, God's life, that flows through us. That reboot is called *salvation* (Luke 1:77) because we are saved from eternal separation from God. It is also called *conversion* (Acts 15:3) because God converts us from being His enemies to being His friends, His allies. It is called *regeneration* (Titus 3:5) because God takes what was "formless and void" (Genesis 1:1-2) and gives it form. He takes the chaos and brings in order, His order. God takes our "nothing" (our paltry efforts to make ourselves good enough before Him) and makes His "something" (pleasing in His sight because of Jesus). In short, we become a "new creation" (2 Corinthians 5:17). It is when we get plugged into our new Life Source that we can get recalibrated. Now we can find our location so that we can calculate our destination. When you are calibrated to God spiritually, the One Who knows the way (John 14:5-6) will get us to the destination we desire.

We just spoke of getting calibrated to God spiritually. How can we recalibrate using the Bible? The Bible establishes your location from the beginning, and your location is Genesis, not your Culture. The first few chapters of Genesis (1-4) are key to all of life. They give us more than a description of how the world and all of life came into being. These chapters direct us to the source of our spiritual life and happiness.

1. *Genesis establishes Authority.* When we accept that the "worlds were prepared by the word of God" (Hebrews 11:3), we accept the fact that God has established Himself as the preeminent authority in the universe. Since "all things came into being through Him" (John 1:3; Genesis 1:1), He is above all earthly and spiritual authority (Psalm 97:9; Ephesians 1:20-21). His word is superseded by no other voice. His word supersedes everything.

2. *Genesis establishes Boundaries.* The bounds of everything that exists provides us with order, stability and meaning. There is order that we can count on because the moon will always be the moon. Rocks will never become trees. Up will always be up, and North will always be North. Because "two plus two equals four," we have stability. We can count on our vehicles getting us where we need to go because the engineers that built them placed their trust in the Truth that God established. We will continue to enjoy the play of children because men have always been

men, and women have always been women. We are living proof that gender is a God-thing. Because we have boundaries we can count on, we have meaning that is attainable. Life has purpose because the Creation that God brought into existence is going somewhere. Because God has given this universe a purpose, our lives have purpose. We are here, under God's authority, to accomplish our part of His plan.

In the final analysis, God really is in the driver's seat. Since His Word is above every other word, we answer to Him. This is the real reason why we read God's Word. When we understand that we belong to Him, we understand that He is the One to direct our lives, not our Culture.

Now, throw Culture into this mix, and you can be sure that there is going to be a struggle. We cannot get away from that. Life is not going to be easy because this world, our Culture, "lies under the power of the evil (wicked) one" (1 John 5:19). That is where the rub comes in.

What are we to do when our culture is in rebellion? Remember, civil authority is an extension of God's authority (Romans 13:1). We are obligated by God to obey civil authority except when it contradicts God's authority (Romans 13:2; Exodus 20:3).

So, when it comes down to the small examples of obeying the posted speed limit and coming to a full stop at a stop sign, we are showing by our behavior that we are under God's authority. There is somebody different talking in our ear and directing our steps. We are listening to an authority, and it is not Culture. It is the Word of God. Now, what others think does not rattle us. All we desire is to find God's grace.

Do we find *grace*? Yes! Because God "resists the proud but gives grace to the humble" (James 4:6; 1 Peter 5:5).

Questions for Group Reflection

1. In your experience, how does your generation define "truth?" Does this definition lean more toward the classical definition of "truth" or toward the modern definition of "preferences?"

2. Consider the navigation app you use for driving or walking. What effect do you think the presence or absence of a biblical starting location will have on your ability to grow deeper in Jesus?

3. Discuss what you understand about God's authority over our lives and God's boundaries for our lives. What effect might the presence or absence of these two concepts have on a person's Christian life? Why might this be an important issue?

4. One way of understanding authentic Christianity is to see it as "counter-cultural." How do you understand Christianity as "counter-cultural?"

5. Read Romans 12:2. Discuss what this says about letting God direct our steps versus letting modern culture dictate to us. What kind of practical examples can you think of to illustrate each concept?

Section Three:
Relational Prayer

Catching Jesus Praying

Charles Haddon Spurgeon (1834–1892) was a Baptist minister who pastored a congregation in England. He is considered one of the most popular preachers of the 19th century. When asked what was more important: prayer or Bible reading, Spurgeon would ask, "What is more important: breathing in or breathing out?" (Crystal Park Baptist Church Benoni).

Three places in the New Testament record Jesus referring to the two greatest commandments upon which hang the whole Law and the prophets. They are found in Matthew 22:35-40, Mark 12:28-34, and Luke 10:25-27. We have previously discussed why we must immerse ourselves in Scripture. It is so that we will come fully under the authority of God, obeying the words of His mouth. A rich relationship with God that is full of spiritual life and energy. It is a relationship marked by the presence of God (Genesis 39:3; Genesis 39:23). A life full of the presence of God is a life characterized by obedience (John 14:15; John 14:23; 1 Samuel 15:22).

When we grow deeper in Jesus, our experience becomes one where we host God's presence (John 14:23). This is not a mind game or theoretical proposition, as Westerners might imagine. This Western idea fits only with an absentee God or distant Father. The ancients of the Bible experienced God as fully integrated with their world. Thus, hosting God's presence was an attainable living reality. In another place (Revelation 3:20), Jesus restated John 14:23 in a different way. You see, hosting God will, of necessity, involve table fellowship. This table fellowship will involve the exchange of conversation. There will be time to hear the words that come from the mouth of our divine Guest (the Word of God). There will also be opportunities to respond to what the Father has expressed (prayer).

We must remember as we think about speaking with God that there is a difference between religion and relation. When we talk about prayer, sometimes we hear of something called "religious prayer." What is a religious prayer?

When two people begin a relationship, there is an inward desire both to know and to be known. Problems develop, however, in this relationship-building process when one or both people construct barriers. When barriers are put up, the true self is often not shown until some time has passed. Why do people construct barriers that prevent another person from knowing them? People raise barriers because they want something from the other person. People hide their flaws so they can appear likable. They want a relationship with the other person, and they fear any flaws will prevent that relationship from continuing. Barriers prevent another person from seeing our real selves because we rationalize if they really knew us, they would not like us. If they do not like us, they will not give us what we want, a relationship with them. Barriers are a tool used to control another person. Religious prayers work the same way. A religious prayer has nothing to do with form. It has everything to do with function.

You will find in some churches that prayers are written and then recited either individually or corporately. Some of the prayers you will hear in churches have high-sounding words that we do not use in everyday speech. That has everything to do with form. A good prayer is not about what words you use or your body position while praying. Social protocols change when you meet your next-door neighbor or good friend, after which you have a meeting with a dignitary like a King or Queen. Keep in mind the function of the prayer. Why (not "how") are you praying? If you are trying to hide your bad self so that God will like you and give you what you want, you are praying a religious prayer. God sees right through that because nothing is hidden from His sight (Jeremiah 16:17). We can try to keep things in the dark when we come to God, but darkness and light are the same to God (Psalm 139:11-12). Religious prayer is an exercise in futility. Religious prayers get us nowhere with God.

If we understand what constitutes a religious prayer, what, then, is a relational prayer? Let us go back to the relationship model described at the beginning of this section. Relationships grow best in an environment of trust. Trust happens when two parties risk opening themselves to the other person. What do they risk? They risk the other person weaponizing the inner person they have shown. It is that inner person that is less than their image of "ideal." Ladies, it involves coming to your man without emotional makeup. Men, it is coming to your lady without sucking in your emotional stomach. This is how you really look, unmasked. Now that is vulnerable! But when two people take that risk, each pledging not to use the other person's weaknesses against them, a foundation of trust, or safety, is laid. It is on this safe foundation that a lasting relationship is built. Now, back to relational prayer. Relational prayer can only happen when we stop pretending with God. We come to Him as we are, admitting our weaknesses and sins, our shortcomings, and our inability to "fix" ourselves. We are indeed in need of grace. We need mercy because we see ourselves as He sees us, without pretense. It is on this trusting foundation that we come. A trusting foundation it is for sure. We are trusting that the God Who knows us will not weaponize our weaknesses against us. And He will not. He remembers that we are "dust" (Psalm 103:14). He is slow to anger and abounding in lovingkindness (Exodus 34:6).

Since we cannot control God, it is pointless to construct relational barriers with Him. He is unpredictable. Because we cannot control or predict God, we "fear" the Lord (Proverbs 14:26). At the same time, we know that He is "good" (Psalm 136:1). So, when we come to Him uncovered, stark naked with our bare faults hanging out, He accepts us and welcomes us just as we are. Because He is good, He does not weaponize our shortcomings. It is in this relationship that we become what we never could be on our own. As we commune with Him in both planned and unplanned appointments, He transforms us. Moses was transformed because he spent time in God's presence (Exodus 34:1-35). We also are transformed as we spend time with God in His presence (2 Corinthians 3:18).

Now, consider Jesus' relationship with God. Before Jesus came to earth as a baby, he had a relationship with God the Father. We read about that relationship in both John chapter 1 and Philippians chapter 2.

Philippians 2:

- v. 6: Jesus existed in the "form of God." In other words, He was an exact duplicate. The writer to the Hebrews compares Jesus with God and says Jesus is "the radiance of His glory and the exact representation of His nature" (Hebrews 1:3). You cannot separate one from the other, and you cannot tell them apart.
- v. 6: Jesus did not consider equality with God as something He was afraid of losing.
- v. 7: Jesus emptied Himself of His prerogatives, entrusting Himself completely to the Father.
- v. 7: Jesus became a human, but not just any human. He became a servant kind of human. That is how much He trusted God His Father. He trusted God would not take advantage of His weakness and vulnerability.

John 1:

- v. 1: Jesus was "the Word," God's utterance that went forth from God and did His bidding.
- v. 2: When God appears out of nowhere (Genesis 1:1), Jesus is there with Him.
- v. 3: Jesus, God's Word, created everything that has ever been created. His hand touched and formed everything.
- v. 4: Jesus brings God's Life to man in a tangible, meaningful way. Here is Jesus, fully human

and fully God, bicultural, at home equally in two worlds. Jesus is at home in the world of eternity as well as the world of created time. He has a trusting relationship with His Father that extends to mortals, you and me.

Because God's Word will not return to God empty-handed (void), He will accomplish everything the Father has sent Him forth to do (Isaiah 55:11). Because Jesus was "with God" and "was God" (John 1:1), He was fully aligned to hear (obey) everything the Father said to Him (Mark 12:29; Deuteronomy 6:4-5).

Before we look at the instances in the Gospels where Jesus uttered prayers, we need to understand something else about Jesus. Most of what we read in the Gospels records what Jesus said and did.

- Jesus did only what He saw the Father doing (John 5:19).
- Jesus spoke only what He heard the Father speaking (John 7:16; 12:49-50; 14:10).

It could very well be that prayer, for Jesus, was communion with his Father as well as to receive instructions for speaking and doing.

Jesus' instruction on prayer is often referred to as The Lord's Prayer. It is one He taught His disciples to pray. But this prayer was not the only prayer Jesus prayed. What we call The Lord's Prayer might be more accurately named, The Disciples' Prayer. Following is a table of prayers Jesus prayed to His Father. This is where we catch Jesus praying.

Table 9 – Catching Jesus Praying

REFERENCE	EVENT	CONTEXT (What else was happening around this event?)
Mark 1:35	Jesus gets up while it is still dark and goes to a solitary place to pray	Just after healing Peter's mother-in-law of a fever and just before going into the surrounding towns and villages speaking of the Kingdom of God
Matthew 11:25-26; Luke 10:21	Praising the Father for hiding "these things" from the wise and revealing them to little children	After "Woes on Unrepentant Cities" and before "Take my yoke upon you"
Luke 6:12	Jesus spends the night in prayer to God	Right after healing the man with a withered hand in the synagogue on the Sabbath and right before calling the Twelve Disciples
Matthew 14:19; Mark 6:41; Luke 9:15; John 6:11	Jesus gives thanks to the Father for the loaves and fish	After John, the Baptist's beheading and just before feeding the crowd of at least 5,000
Matthew 14:22-23	Jesus withdraws to a solitary place to pray	After feeding the 5,000 and before walking on water in the storm.
Matthew 15:35-36; Mark 8:7	Jesus blesses the Father for providing the loaves and fish	After the faith of the Canaanite woman and just before feeding of the crowd of at least 4,000
John 11:41-42	Jesus thanks the Father for hearing Him	After the death of His friend, Lazarus, and just before the plots to kill Jesus
Matthew 26:26; Mark 14:22-23	Jesus blesses the Father for providing the bread and the wine	During the Last Supper and just before going to the Mount of Olives
John 17:1-5	Jesus prays for Himself	Just after speaking to the disciples about the work of the Holy Spirit, and just before going to the Garden of Gethsemane
John 17:6-19	Jesus prays for His disciples	Just after speaking to the disciples about the work of the Holy Spirit, and just before going to the Garden of Gethsemane
John 17:20-26	Jesus prays for all the future Children of God	Just after speaking to the disciples about the work of the

John 17:20-26	Jesus prays for all the future Children of God	Just after speaking to the disciples about the work of the Holy Spirit, and just before going to the Garden of Gethsemane
Matthew 26:39-42; Mark 14:35-39; Luke 22:41	Jesus prays to the Father in the Garden of Gethsemane	Just after the Last Supper and before His arrest, trial, and crucifixion
Luke 23:34	Jesus asks the Father to forgive those crucifying Him	After His trial and before His death.
Matthew 27:45; Mark 15:33	Jesus asks the Father why He has been forsaken	During the crucifixion, just after His trial and just before His death
Luke 24:30	Jesus gives thanks over bread while dining with the two disciples He met on the road to Emmaus	After His resurrection, before His appearance to the eleven disciples

Before we observe some specific things about Jesus' prayers, let us remember some things about Jesus in His Middle Eastern setting.

- The group was more important than the individual.
- "Honor" and "shame" were the main driving forces. "Glory"/"glorify" was a synonym for "honor."
- God was the Patron, and Jesus was the Broker ("Friend") for the good riches of the kingdom of heaven.

Now, notice some things about the prayers of Jesus.

- Of all these recorded prayers, only one (John 17:1-5, five verses) is about Himself. In this prayer, Jesus asks the Father to increase His honor ("glorify"). This is not for His own benefit, but rather that He may, in turn, bring honor to the Father.

- In His prayer over food, Jesus blessed God in the traditional Hebrew way. He did not ask God to "bless the food." Rather, the ancient Hebrew prayer probably went something like this: "Blessed art thou, O Lord our God, King of the universe, who bringest forth bread from the earth" (Hertz, The Authorized Daily Prayer Book, 963).

The central focus of this kind of prayer is not the request itself but rather the recognition of the goodness and faithfulness of God.

- Jesus' major emphasis in John 17 seems to be "the group." He uses five verses to pray for Himself, fourteen verses to pray for His disciples, and then seven verses praying for believers everywhere. This is the kind of "other" focus that supports what Jesus said was the second greatest command: loving one's neighbor (Matthew 22:39). When a person wonders how their needs will be met, this "other" focus promotes trust in the following ways:
  o we remember that there are "others" who are praying for us, and
  o we remember that God is mindful of our needs and has the resources to meet those needs (Matthew 6:25-34).

Questions for Group Reflection

1. Consider the quote by Charles Haddon Spurgeon. How do you think Bible reading and prayer relate to breathing in and breathing out? How do you think the absence of either of those activities would affect your spiritual life?

2. Compare the American view of an "absentee" God who we beg to intervene in everyday life with the ancient view of a fully "integrated" God who has no need to intervene. What kind of shift does the Ancient view bring to the subject of answered prayer?

3. After reading the difference between "religious prayer" and "relational prayer," discuss how these two types of prayer might play out in a person's prayer life. What types of things might a person want to hide while praying a "religious prayer?"

4. Read Matthew 6:10 and then re-read the section, "Jesus' Relationship with God the Father." Now, compare Jesus' prayer in Matthew 6:10 with what He said He spoke and did in John 5:19 and John 14:10. How is Jesus' prayer in Matthew 6:10 answered in John 5:19 and John 14:10? How does Jesus' prayer in Matthew 6:10 compare to the much of the subject content of our prayers?

5. The subject content of much American praying that I am familiar with has much to do with "me" and "mine." Discuss why you think it is so difficult to make the majority of our prayers about the needs of others? If I am going to get my needs prayed for by my neighbor, what must I do, and how risky is that? Why is it so hard to be truly known by another person? What makes this level of vulnerability hard for me? What makes this level of vulnerability hard for the person who hears me? (i.e., What kind of internal feelings are triggered in me and the other person when I become vulnerable with that other person?)

6. Discuss what you think the person requesting prayer and the person hearing that vulnerability will need to work on individually in order to grow relationally with each other and spiritually with God.

Kingdom Relationship Brings Kingdom Direction

One of the hardest things for an American to understand is the concept of the kingdom of heaven or the kingdom of God. Why is that? We have a cultural conundrum.

When the New Testament speaks of the kingdom of heaven, it is not speaking of heaven, the believer's eternal home. When modern Westerners speak of heaven, our final destination is often what we speak of. The ancient understanding found in the Bible is much different. The biblical emphasis is on the kingdom that emanates from the highest known place a person can imagine, heaven. This is how our cultural differences give us such problems.

When "kingdom" is described in the Bible using the lofty prepositional phrase, "of heaven," this kingdom is set apart from all other known kingdoms. *Heaven* is a substitute for the name *God*. God, the ruler of heaven, is the authority above every other authority. When you get to God, there is no second opinion. When you arrive at heaven, you have arrived at the supreme court of the Universe. The decision that comes down from there supersedes every other ruling and mandate. The kingdom of heaven is the place from which the final verdict comes.

When a person speaks of the "kingdom of heaven," that person is really speaking of spiritual authority. Spiritual authority is ultimately not rooted in the leadership of a church. Church leaders are merely an extension of God's authority and are answerable to God for how they treat their fellow "kingdom citizens."

When modern Americans read the biblical phrase, "the fear of the LORD" (Job 28:28; Psalm 19:9; Psalm 111:10; Proverbs 9:10), they typically make the word "fear" synonymous with the word "respect." We have difficulty thinking about fearing God when Scripture tells us we are to love God (Deuteronomy 6:5; Luke 10:27).

Americans have gotten so accustomed to a representative republic form of government that it is extremely difficult to imagine what life was like when one person held all the power. One must go back several centuries to the kings and queens of Europe before that kind of authority is found. There were no branches of government or separation of powers in ancient kingdoms. The king or queen was answerable only to themselves. Lewis Carroll's children's fiction story *Through the Looking-Glass* was a living nightmare if you lived under a wicked king or queen. "Off with her head!" was a command that struck terror. There was no recourse in this situation. This kind of power was a power unchallenged by few and overwhelming to most. It was the kind of power that made people live with a view to survive the present because the future was not guaranteed. If you lived under the rule of an evil king or queen, you could not predict with any certainty either the quality or length of your life. You feared the monarch because the monarch was unpredictable. Your fortunes depended on his or her emotional state. This was the kind of king Herod the Great was at the time of the birth of Jesus Christ.

When the Bible speaks of the "fear of the LORD," it is this kind of fear that it references. This is not the kind of "respect" that Americans think of when they call a person by the honorific title of "Mr.," "Mrs.," "Dr.," "Lady," or "Lord." When we read the word "fear" in the Old Testament coupled with the phrase "of the LORD," the general understanding of this word is simply fear. The emotion one has before a monarch translates to a posture of great humility. Humble people fall down on their knees or prostrate themselves face down before this majesty. They do not want to do or say anything that would move them from friend to adversary. This is the kind of fear Jesus referenced when He said in Matthew 10:28, "Do not be afraid of those who kill the body but cannot kill the soul. Rather, be afraid of the One who can destroy both soul and body in hell." This is the kind of fear that regulates how one lives before the King of the Universe and appears before Him. Because of God's unrestrained power, one does not live before God or appear before God either casually or indifferently. One pays attention. It is because one understands this concept that one gains wisdom (Psalm 111:10) and seeks to detach themselves from evil (Proverbs 16:6).

The first understanding a person needs to internalize is this concept of "fear" that is founded upon unrestrained and overwhelming power. This is part of the reason why a Christian must find their foundation in Genesis chapters 1-4. The second understanding a person must internalize is the goodness and grace of God's character.

The balance to this unimaginable might is God's character. How did God reveal Himself to Moses when Moses wanted to see God's glory? Exodus 34:6-7 says,

And he passed in front of Moses, proclaiming, "The LORD, the LORD, the compassionate and gracious God, slow to anger, abounding in love and faithfulness, maintaining love to thousands, and forgiving wickedness, rebellion and sin. Yet he does not leave the guilty unpunished; he punishes the children and their children for the sin of the parents to the third and fourth generation."

The designation "LORD God" is first found in Genesis 2:4. Rabbinic commentators speak of these two names in the following way. "God" (Hebrew *Elohim*) refers to a "God of Judgment." "LORD" (Hebrew *Hashem*, also written *Adonai*) refers to a "God of Mercy" (Zlotowitz, *Bereishis / Genesis*, 87).

When God works with the raw materials, He is slicing and dicing. But when God begins to refine things and then brings mankind into the mix, mercy is introduced. God describes His character of mercy in Exodus 34:6-7 as "compassionate and gracious," "slow to anger, abounding in love and faithfulness," "maintaining love to thousands, and forgiving wickedness, rebellion and sin."

It is this character quality of "LORD" that mitigates or softens the hardness of fear. The "Fear" of God is the "slicing-and-dicing"—the "God" (Elohim) part. You do not want to mess with that or treat that lightly! But when the Lord actually touches our being, what we experience is His compassion, grace, love, and faithfulness.

Since we are living now after the events of the crucifixion and resurrection of Jesus, it is this "LORD" part of God's character that we experience in Jesus. The apostle John said of Jesus, "we have seen his glory...full of grace and truth" (John 1:14). This is also why the apostle Paul could write that God calls us into His "kingdom and glory" (1 Thessalonians 2:12). The apostle Paul also blessed the churches in his greetings with "grace and peace to you from God our Father and from the Lord Jesus Christ" (Romans 1:7; 1 Corinthians 1:3; 2 Corinthians 1:2; Galatians 1:3; Ephesians 1:2). You see, "grace and peace" are how we get to experience the kingdom of God, all because of our experience with Jesus.

It is this kingdom relationship that brings kingdom direction. The lordship of Jesus (grace, peace, and faithfulness) is anchored in His divinity. He is God (Elohim). Remember the final words of God to Moses in His self-revelation? "He does not leave the guilty unpunished" (Exodus 34:7). This is the element of "fear" that we cannot lose. You just cannot predict or control God. He is His own Person. And what about us? When we keep in mind the "fear of the LORD," this causes us to approach Him in humility. We have nothing to boast about. We have no standing in His courtroom. There is nothing we can do to improve our lot before Him. We are totally at His mercy. But just when we fear the worst, we get the best. He holds out His scepter to us, and we approach, touching the end of His scepter, receiving life from Him instead of death.

Now that we understand our relationship to Him, we are ready to receive His royal direction. This direction is not arbitrary. It comes from the high court of the universe. He commands, and we obey.

This is our experience when we approach God in the attitude of relational prayer.

Questions for Group Reflection

1. Discuss what you have been taught in Christian circles about what the "fear of the Lord" means. Using that definition, how do you think that would work out in real life? How do you "do that?"

2. Now, compare what you read in the section entitled, "Fear Versus Respect." Why do you think many Christians have such a problem with actually "fearing" God? What is it that they do not grasp about God's character?

3. Compare Psalm 136:1 with Matthew 7:18. Now discuss this question: "Is it possible for God to ever be bad or do bad things?" If the answer your group came up with is "yes," where do you think this answer is coming from? Does it come from our Culture or from Scripture? (When you answer this question about culture, consider how insurance companies designate catastrophic storms that take lives and destroy property.) Why do you think it is sometimes so hard to trust God's character?

4. God's kingdom rule (authority) flows out of God's character. If we do not trust that God is essentially good, how will that distrust affect a person submitting themselves to God's authority?

5. Discuss as a group whether you think a person can be a Christian without submitting to the authority of God. What do you think is the difference between being "religious" and being "Christian?"

6. Read Isaiah 14:12-14. Discuss what you think the spiritual issue is that causes people to resist the idea of submitting themselves to the authority of God. What do you think the remedy is for this? Why should we submit ourselves to God? Why is this such a different message from what our American culture tells us? What must we do to work humility into our lives?

Models of Prayer for Every Need

We are talking about the broad subject of relational prayer. A growing relationship with another person requires the give-and-take of communication. When no special needs present themselves, we might safely say that a growing, healthy relationship needs healthy conversation. For many people, prayer consists of the pray-er doing all the talking and God doing all the listening. After all, isn't God is the silent partner in this relationship? Well, not exactly. Even in a relationship where one person has been silenced because of tragedy or illness, if that person is at all coherent, there is still a back-and-forth, giving-and-receiving interaction that goes on between the two individuals. Somehow, each one has input, and so the relationship grows. If I am doing all the talking in my prayer life and then getting up and moving on with my life, there is no relational growth taking place between God and me.

Prayer is supposed to be a sharing of life between me and God across the great divide that separates time from eternity. If I do all the talking and do not wait for my Father to respond, I have just finished a monologue. I have not yet prayed. I must give my life to Him in prayer and then receive His Life (divine energy) as the resource I need to handle life's challenges.

But sometimes, it is hard to start what we feel will be a difficult conversation with God. It is in these situations that we desperately long for an icebreaker. Have you ever gone to a gathering of people where you knew you would be with strangers? Do you remember how you felt? Maybe you are a social butterfly by nature, so it really did not bother you. Maybe you are a clown by nature and enjoy entertaining and watching people laugh. If those two types of people describe you, then you understand why crowds and strangers do not pose a threat. You always seem to have a few wisecracks at the ready to get the party started. Maybe you look forward to warming up to people and making new friends.

But then, maybe you are a little like me. I find it easy to stand on the sidelines and observe. I am what some would call an introvert. It is so easy to pull my head into my shell, followed by my arms and legs. Life is better at a party when you are a turtle! I will come out if someone knocks on my shell. Yes, that is my superpower! If you want me to interact with complete strangers, you really need to come up with some icebreakers. Icebreakers have a way of cracking through the coldness of the room and opening channels of communication and connection where before there were none.

Sometimes prayer to God feels like this. God is just so...strange and off-ish! Get in an enclosed space with God, and it is easier to just fade into the scenery. Well, with God, that does not work. The whole earth is full of His glory (Isaiah 6:3). There is no place we can go, whether in an enclosed or open space, where we cannot bump into God (Psalms 139:7-10).

Since God is everywhere, we might as well figure out how to talk to Him. It might be helpful to think of God as a person you are walking beside or sitting beside. The rabbis had a saying about discipleship and following a rabbi: "Yose ben Yoezer, leader of Tz'redah, says: Let your house be a meeting place for Torah scholars; you shall become dusty in the dust of their feet; and you shall drink in their words thirstily" (Lieber, *The Pirkei Avos Treasury*, 21).

For the Jews, when you are in a discipleship relationship with a spiritual mentor, you are to walk so closely to them that the dust on the pathway stirred up by their feet sticks to you. You get dusty because of your close relationship. Guess what? In that kind of close relationship, you talk about...everything!

Another way to think about conversation starters with God comes from sitting around either a firepit or campfire. When a log is added to the fire and begins burning, embers are sometimes seen ascending in the smoke. Prayer is like that. What kind of log do you have on the hearth of your heart? Whatever it is, open your chimney and let the sparks of those concerns or joys fly upward! You and God are sitting there together. Show Him what you have inside! If you try to close things off, your emotions will end up burning you up on the inside (Psalm 39:3).

One of the great things about reading the Bible is that as you read, different people introduce you to different models of prayer. One of the best places to look when a person wants to learn how to pray is the Bible. Just observe these people and watch how they interacted with God. They did not mess around, they got real in a hurry! And what do you know: God responded! The Bible is full of people's interactions with God, the conversations we label as prayer. Here are a few examples.

Adam: "Over here, God, among the trees. I was naked so I was afraid to come out when you called." (Genesis 3:8-10). Well, that is embarrassing! Still, Adam offered it up, and God accepted his praying and the place from which he prayed. Adam, in this prayer, is admitting sin. But God has grace to cover that sin.

Abraham: "Bahahaha! Good one, God! Do you really think an old guy like me can make a baby? You have got to be kidding!" (Genesis 17:1-17). Wow! Here is the man that embodies faith to us, hanging out all his doubts for everybody to see! Who in their right mind hangs out their dirty laundry? But look how gentle God is with him. God does not berate Abraham or put him down. God just walks with Abraham while Abraham grows his faith. Wow!

Moses: "I am so mad I could spit!" (Numbers 11:10-17). Well, sometimes enough is enough. You just cannot take it anymore! That is where Moses was at this point. All that toxicity on the inside just came right out, and it was not pretty! You know what? God is big enough that He can handle that. Not only did God handle it, but God gave Moses a way out so he could handle it too.

David: David gives us several examples of prayer. (1) "Strike them and scatter them, God!" (Psalm 68:1). (2) "God, I just love spending time in Your Word!" (my re-phrase of Psalm 119:97). (3) "God, Help me! Look how far I have fallen!" (Psalm 51:1-19). David is a wonderful prayer instructor because he is all over the map. In Psalms, David goes from a clenched fist and gritted teeth, to rapturous joy, to deep sorrow for sin. You know what? God loves it! God calls David a "man after His own heart" (1 Samuel 13:14).

Hannah: "God, my pain is so deep I can't even give it a voice!" (1 Samuel 1:3-15). When her pastor (Eli, the priest) heard Hannah pray this prayer, he misunderstood what was going on and rebuked her. That was like adding salt to her heart wound. God did not misunderstand or rebuke. God turned that around and gave her peace and the answer to her heart's longing.

Jesus: Jesus, like David, gives us more than one example of prayer. (1) "God, I just *love* the way You are working!" (my rephrase of Matthew 11:25). (2) "God, I do not like the way You're working one bit! Can't we do something different here?" (my rephrase of Luke 22:42). God loved hearing Jesus pray (Hebrews 5:7) because Jesus said what He felt, and He was totally committed to doing God's will. A prayer in that attitude is powerful (1 John 5:14-15).

Stephen: "God, be merciful to them! They do not know what they are doing!" (Acts 7:54-60). While he was being put to death for a so-called "crime," Stephen, a church deacon, prayed this! Doesn't that prayer sound a lot like Jesus? Yes. But that is the point of walking with Jesus. We are supposed to sound and act more and more like Him!

Paul: "God, help your people grow in you!" (Ephesians 3:16-17). Here is another prayer that is according to the will of God (Romans 8:29). Any prayer that lines up with the will of God is powerful and effective (1 John

5:14-15). Another reason why this kind of prayer is powerful is that it is "neighbor-focused." When we relate positively to our neighbors, God pays attention.

I hope this has helped you put a face to the name called prayer. Prayer is not some pretty language, razzle-dazzle monologue that somebody unearths from the Middle Ages in King James English.

Prayer is just living out of the depths, the guts, of life in front of our Creator. Prayer is recognizing that God is either standing, or sitting, or lying in the space beside us. He has taken up residence with us. His name is Immanuel, God with us (Matthew 1:23). Prayer recognizes this reality and welcomes His presence in everyday living and dying. This is the reason we pray "without ceasing" (1 Thessalonians 5:17).

Questions for Group Reflection

1. How difficult is it for you to engage with others in a group? What kinds of perceptions of others either help you connect or keep you in your shell?

2. On a scale of 1–10, with 1 being really easy and 10 being really hard, how difficult would you say it is for you to verbalize prayer aloud to God? What perceptions of others either encourage you to verbalize or cause you to stay silent?

3. Looking at the models of prayer listed above, what prayer were you most comfortable with? Now, what prayer were you least comfortable with? Why do you feel that is so?

4. Out of the model prayers listed above, which prayer sounds most like you? Why do you feel that? If none of the prayers listed above sound like a prayer you would pray, what other prayer in the Bible sounds like you? Why do you feel that?

5. Discuss why you think it is so hard for people to get really honest and open with God. Now read aloud Exodus 34:6-7, followed by Romans 8:1. How would you use these two verses to encourage a person to get real with God?

God's Will Versus My Wants

I am writing this chapter during a quiet day. It is Saturday, the day between Good Friday and Easter Sunday, 2020. The whole world is experiencing the grip of COVID-19, the novel Coronavirus. To date, hundreds of thousands worldwide have been infected. As of this writing, on April 11, 2020, there are over 1 million 700 thousand confirmed worldwide cases, over 100 thousand deaths, and over 400 thousand people recovered (Worldometer, "COVID-19 Coronavirus Pandemic," 2020). Because of social distancing during this pandemic, the world has gotten quieter...much quieter. Seismologists have noted that since various urban centers of the world have issued stay-at-home orders, the world's normal noise level has been significantly reduced. Now, earthquake rumblings of "middling magnitudes emanating from distant continents" can be heard in London, all because the world's normal activity has grown silent (Andrews, "Coronavirus Turns Urban Life's Roar to Whisper on World's Seismographs," 2020).

While millions in Africa and India wonder whether they will be able to eat another meal because they cannot store food, Americans are anxious over the shortage of toilet paper. This difference highlights a conspicuous fact: Americans are predominantly consumers.

A consumer mentality drives the American economy. Americans buy things to use and then discard. There have not been significant disturbing shortages until now. By comparison, the current level of various shortages seems to have eclipsed the gasoline shortages of the 1970s. The national anxiety level somehow feels greater. Isn't there always more somewhere? That "more" may be product or money. It does not matter. When you are a consumer, you usually find a way to get more when you run out. This is the comfort Americans have gotten accustomed to over the past 60 years. Now, we are no longer comfortable. Now, we wonder what we will do when we run out of...toilet paper.

A consumer mentality appears to find its center in the individual. That really fits the Western mindset. Americans seemed focused on themselves. When the culture is observed as a whole, from top-to-bottom, "self" and "what is in it for me" appear to decide why we choose our paths.

This is evident in modern culture, but unfortunately, it is also evident in Christian circles. Why do people change churches? Many times, the reason comes down to what a person is not receiving rather than the lack of opportunity to give and so contribute to the welfare of the group.

God's driving narrative, His storyline, is to improve the lot of the "other." Who is the "other?" The one outside of Himself. It is the one God is separated (holy) from. God begins by creating mankind in a male-and-female variety. He gives them everything they need to flourish. Then, when they walk away, God gives Himself.

Remember our narrative about Bible words? Remember the colors culture paints words with? The *individualist* culture understands "love" to be something the "self" feels and enjoys. The collective culture understands "love" to be an attachment to another person to build up the collective group.

When we come to one of the most famous verses of the Bible, John 3:16, we discover the depth of God's driving narrative.

Reinterpreted from the collectivist perspective, John 3:16 might read: "For God so loved [*attached Himself to*] the world, that He gave His only begotten son, [*the Man-child Who was God incarnate*] that whosoever believes in [*commits himself totally and without reservation to and attaches himself to*] Him shall not perish [*be totally separated from*] but have everlasting life [*the God-life that attaches him to God forever*]" (Italicized additions in this verse are mine).

God's driving narrative inserts God in person into the story of man for the good and best outcome of mankind. That is a huge risk! It risks rejection, which is exactly what happened at the crucifixion. Man rejected the God-man. But just when the story could not get any worse, it got better. God's power overcame rejection and the ultimate of separations, death, with resurrection. There is no better story than that, and there is no better proof that God's strength and might are greater than the greatest power that can bind a person in individual isolation. Whatever you may have going on, just remember: God is bigger than that!

Many at the time of this writing are experiencing isolation. There are mandates in many areas of America that require people to stay home. This is a nationwide effort to curtail the spread of COVID-19. In a sense, we are all isolated. Isolation is the destination of individualism. We are barred from going to sporting events. We cannot socialize at restaurants. Christians, for the first time in America's history, will watch an Easter church service televised into the comforts of their living room. Isolation is lonely. For many, isolation is hell on earth.

God's will for mankind is not isolation. It is integration. God is a Master at bringing opposing parties together. With God's intervention, there are new beginnings that blossom into new relationships. God and man come together. When God and man come together, man and neighbor come together.

How does all this relate to relational prayer? When I "want what I want when I want it," I am being governed by my culture. I am consumer-driven. But when I am looking out for my neighbor, suddenly I recognize the Life of God that is bursting forth from my innermost being like a fountain. This is God at work, wanting the best for my neighbor. This is God at work, seeking to integrate through me with my neighbor to form a new community. God is at work! When God begins working, the death of isolation, that living hell, is cast off. A new relationship can begin because of God's resurrection life!

When I begin to pray for *all* my neighbors, my prayers include my enemies. This is God's greatest work! How do I destroy my enemies? I make them my friends. How do I make them my friends? When I pray for my enemies, God begins revealing to me their needs. Once I recognize their needs, I can humble myself to meet them. Suddenly the handcuffs of a broken relationship begin to loosen. With continued kindness without any expectation of return, the key that sets the prisoner, that enemy, free also unlocks the door to my heart and releases the pent-up feelings of bitterness.

Is this kind of loving and living risky business? Absolutely! I risk having my overtures for a life-giving relationship rebuffed. So, what happens if my enemy, having had his cell door unlocked with an offer of freedom, chooses to close the barred door and remain imprisoned? There is still one person in this relationship that walks out of the prison house. That person is me.

You see, when I prayed relationally for my enemy, God handed me the key to the cell door that kept me prisoner. I then used the key God gave me to not only unlock my door but also open the door imprisoning my enemy. If my enemy chooses to walk out of the jailhouse with me, we can both begin a new and different relationship together. If my enemy chooses to stay imprisoned, I can still walk out the front door of that prison compound a free man.

That is the power of *relational prayer*.

Questions for Group Reflection

1. Discuss in your group American consumerism versus God's driving narrative in the Bible as it relates to the subject of prayer. Why do you think many Christians struggle with seeing answers to prayer?

2. Look again at God's driving narrative. Consider John 3:16 through the collectivist lens. How does this differ from understanding this verse through the American culture's individualist lens?

3. Read the section regarding God's will again. How does this relate to the subject of unforgiveness? Why do you think Christians in America feel the task of finding God's will so difficult? What do you think needs to change so that finding God's will becomes simple?

4. Discuss in this group how we can make our enemies our friends. What needs to happen on our end? What needs to happen on our enemy's side? How does Matthew 18:21-22 figure into this? What do Jesus' words in this Scripture say about the condition of our heart toward our neighbor? Since Jesus said what the Father told Him to say (John 14:10), what does Matthew 18:21-22

say about the heart of God when we hurt Him repeatedly?

5. Discuss the relationship between "forgiveness" and "consequences." How do you think it is possible to forgive a person for a horrific crime, yet state or federal law requires that person to still serve prison time? What good is forgiveness in this instance?

6. Reflect on this question: "Are there prayers you think God will not respond to?" Now discuss why this is so or why this is not the case.

Section Four:

Not Without My Neighbor

Love and Solidarity

They probably looked like a group of boys huddled together whispering to each other.

"*Ask* him!"

"Not me! *You* ask him!"

"No! *You* are the one that had the question. *You* ask him!"

"Okay! If you insist! I *will* ask him!"

Matthew 22:34-36: "Hearing that Jesus had silenced the Sadducees, the Pharisees got together. One of them, an expert in the law, tested him with this question: 'Teacher, which is the greatest commandment in the Law?'"

You have to love how Jesus answered questions. Sometimes He would answer just the question you asked. Sometimes He asked you a question in return, and if you answered His question, then He would answer yours. Then sometimes...Jesus would give you what you wanted and then give you *more* than you asked for. This was one of *those* times!

> Jesus replied: "'Love the LORD your God with all your heart and with all your soul and with all your mind.' This is the first and greatest commandment. And the second is like it: 'Love your neighbor as yourself.' All the Law and the Prophets hang on these two commandments."
>
> Matthew 22:37-40

Okay. I get it. Jesus first went to Deuteronomy 6:5 for the greatest commandment. This comes straight from the Shema the Jews quoted morning and evening. "Hear, O Israel! The LORD our God! The LORD is One! You shall love the LORD your God with all your heart and with all your soul and with all your might." Jesus answered the great and foremost commandment.

But why talk about the second best? To answer this question, we must understand the setting in which Jesus answered these men. This question was asked by Pharisees in Jerusalem because this event in Matthew chapter 22 happened right after Jesus' Triumphal Entry into Jerusalem in Matthew chapter 21.

The Jerusalem of Jesus' time could be classified as a "preindustrial city" (Malina, *The New Testament World:*

Insights from Cultural Anthropology, 90). In Jesus' day, you had the regular people who lived out in the countryside. They often congregated in villages and lived off the land. They were either farmers or livestock herders, mostly sheep and goats. All these people lived outside the walls of the preindustrial city. Then you had the people inside the walls of the city. In the heart of the city near the Temple or the housing for the Roman ruler lived the elites. This small group was comprised of either the priests or Jewish religious leaders (Sadducees and Herodians) or the Roman rulers or prefects (either one of the Herods or Pontus Pilate). Finally, outside of this elite circle lived and worked the artisans. They were the skilled tradespeople who looked after the needs of the elite and managed the markets and stalls. The elite were made up of about two percent of the population, with the artisans comprising about eight percent of the population. This means that 90 percent of the population of the nation lived outside of the city walls (Malina, *The New Testament World: Insights from Cultural Anthropology*, 91–92).

With both the religious authorities insisting on annual taxes in accordance with the Torah and the Romans insisting on taxes in accordance with Caesar, one understands that the tax burden fell most heavily on the 90 percent, the poorest of the land. What happened if you could not pay?

The inability to pay in a culture of "limited good" guaranteed a life of suffering. Suffering took on the form of debt. If a debtor could not pay what he owed, he was either put in prison or sold into slavery. If prison were the route, his family would be forced to cough up the money in the amount of the debt owed to gain the release of the prisoner. If slavery was the answer, often, the whole family went into slavery, thus forfeiting their land. Who got the land? The elites, of course. So, the rich got richer at the expense of their neighbor, and the poor became poorer because the rich coveted their goods (Neyrey, Jerome H. and Eric C. Stewart. "Economics," 63).

This is the reason Jesus spoke to the religious rulers about loving their neighbors, their brothers in the faith of Abraham. This is also why John the Baptist spoke to those religious rulers about their need for repentance. They needed a behavioral change, a change that could only come from putting the Torah into practice.

Before we can understand how to love our neighbor, we must first answer the question posed to Jesus by the Pharisee, "Who is my neighbor?" Americans are strong individualists but have weak group ties. To an American, the word "neighbor" elicits thoughts of a person living next door or just down the street. A neighbor might even be a person with a disabled vehicle on the side of the road. Usually, the word "neighbor" means "another individual who is unrelated to me."

Middle Easterners thought differently. The people of the Bible had strong group ties that overruled any thoughts of individual achievement. Therefore, the word "neighbor" meant a person of one's immediate family, extended family, clan, tribe, or nation. If you have something in common with another person, they will call you their "brother" or maybe "cousin." These words do not mean that you share a common parent with that person. It simply means that they consider you a member of their group. You are an "insider." This "Eastern" mindset is as true in West Africa as it was to Bible people. I have, on numerous occasions, shared with West Africans where I lived in Nigeria and the foods I enjoyed. Suddenly, with joy on their face, they exclaimed, "You are my brother!" Suddenly, I was no longer an outsider. They considered me part of their group.

In the pages of the Bible, the person receiving alms (donations or help) was a member of one's group (immediate family, extended family, clan, tribe, etc.) that had fallen on hard times (Pilch, *Handbook of Biblical Social Values*, "Altruism: Almsgiving"). With the collectivist worldview, the individual's fortunes fall when the group falls, and the group is diminished when a single member is diminished.

This is the reason why compassion was such a big deal in the Bible. In the American mind, the word "compassion" is often linked to the word "pity." When a person has pity on another, there is sometimes an urge to relieve the suffering of the "other." But sometimes, the thought, *I am glad that is not me!* is all that pity produces. You see, "pity" is typically emotionally distant from suffering. The emotional component is what separates pity from empathy. Empathy comes near the suffering person and shares the burden. Often, empathy is the emotion that compels a person to get their hands dirty, helping a person get unstuck. Empathy has more in common with compassion than pity.

In the Old Testament, the Hebrew word "compassion" is actually a derivative of the Hebrew word "womb" (Pilch, *Handbook of Biblical Social Values*, "Compassion"). This is not to say that compassion is the emotion that a parent shows the child. Rather, this emotion is what siblings of the same womb are to show each other. This is firmly in keeping with the collectivist worldview. If you were a member of the group, you were a neighbor who could receive help. You were shown compassion because you were a brother.

Having identified our neighbor, we must now turn to the means of giving aid. How was someone supposed to "love" their neighbor? To understand this, one needs to understand something of the patriarchal system in which the Middle Easterner lived (Vander Laan, "Israel's Mission with Ray Vander Laan Session One"). The patriarch of the family was given the responsibility of meeting the needs and seeking the well-being of everyone in the family. If a member of the family became excluded for some reason from the "father's house," it was the duty of the patriarch, the father, to redeem that distant person back to the safety and care of the "father's house."

In the case of the Jewish people, God was the Patriarch, and they, as God's representatives on earth, had been given the responsibility of caring for their fellow Jews. To allow a fellow Jew to fall on hard times, or to be the one responsible for creating those hard times, put your status as a bona fide family member in doubt. It was this "family" question that Jesus had in mind in the following Scripture section:

> Jesus replied, "Very truly I tell you, everyone who sins is a slave to sin. Now a slave has no permanent place in the family, but a son belongs to it forever. So if the Son sets you free, you will be free indeed. I know that you are Abraham's descendants. Yet you are looking for a way to kill me, because you have no room for my word. I am telling you what I have seen in the Father's presence, and you

are doing what you have heard from your father." "Abraham is our father," they answered. "If you were Abraham's children," said Jesus, "then you would do what Abraham did. As it is, you are looking for a way to kill me, a man who has told you the truth that I heard from God. Abraham did not do such things. You are doing the works of your own father." "We are not illegitimate children," they protested. "The only Father we have is God himself." Jesus said to them, "If God were your Father, you would love me, for I have come here from God. I have not come on my own; God sent me. Why is my language not clear to you? Because you are unable to hear what I say. You belong to your father, the devil, and you want to carry out your father's desires. He was a murderer from the beginning, not holding to the truth, for there is no truth in him. When he lies, he speaks his native language, for he is a liar and the father of lies.

John 8:34-44

Jesus called into question the religious leaders' patronage because they were doing the same things the prophets had accused them of. Jesus was familiar with the prophet Isaiah when that prophet wrote:

When you spread out your hands in prayer, I
hide my eyes from you; even when you offer
many prayers, I am not listening. Your hands
are full of blood! Wash and make yourselves
clean. Take your evil deeds out of my sight;
stop doing wrong. Learn to do right; seek justice. Defend the oppressed. Take up the cause
of the fatherless; plead the case of the widow.

Isaiah 1:15-17

The Jewish religious leaders of Jesus' day were not
learning to do good. They were not seeking justice.
They were not reproving the ruthless; neither did they
defend the orphan or plead for the widow. They just
kept placing burdens on the people that were not able
to bear them.

It was clear they did not love their neighbor!

This is the social milieu in which the Parable of the
Lost Son is set. Jesus tells this parable in Luke 15:11-32.

As the story goes in the parable, a father had two
sons. The younger son demanded his inheritance from
his father before his father's death. The father divided
his inheritance between his two sons. The younger son
went to a far country and wasted his inheritance, while
the older son stayed with the father, tending the animals. The younger son eventually returned home and

was joyfully reunited with his father. But when the father organized a big party, the older son/older brother refused to participate. The parable ended with the father giving a valid reason for his great joy. "Because this brother of yours was dead and is alive again; he was lost and is found" (Luke 15:32).

Here are some observations from this parable, accounting for the patriarchal system.

1. When the father divided his inheritance between his two sons, he gave the older son two-thirds of the inheritance while the younger son got one-third of the inheritance. What was he doing at this point? The father was, in effect, making the older brother the patriarch of the family, giving him the responsibility of caring for each member (Vander Laan, ibid.).

2. Since this was a patriarchal system and the father was the one responsible for redeeming lost members of the family, why did the father in this parable merely stay at home and wait for the youngest son's return? Because when he divided his inheritance, he also gave the responsibility of redemption to the older son.

3. When the older son complained at the end of the parable of working like a slave and bitterly resented the extravagance of the party for his

younger brother by exclaiming, "Well! You never did that for me," what was he admitting to? When the older son had received two-thirds of his father's inheritance, he received a trust. That trust was to be used for the safe-keeping and well-being of the whole family. Did the older brother use any of his inheritance to redeem his brother? No. Did the older brother use any of his inheritance to feast with his fellow laborers? Apparently not. What did he do? Rather than wisely managing the estate of another (his father), he foolishly treated it as though it was his own, and he felt no obligation to find his lost brother.

The older brother, by not showing solidarity with his brother (from the same father), showed that he really was not a son, even though he lived in the same house as the father.

Loving God requires connections with God's other children. Because of our participation in the Family of God, we must look after the well-being of other members of God's family. This is "loving my neighbor." We have been given the "ministry of reconciliation" (2 Corinthians 5:18) as the apostle Paul has declared. That means we are responsible to live in solidarity with our neighbor. The death and resurrection of Christ give us that responsibility.

Questions for Group Reflection

1. Compare in a group discussion the Western understanding of "loving my neighbor" with the Middle Eastern understanding of "loving my neighbor." If you are wearing Western shoes, how would you love your neighbor? If you are wearing Middle Eastern shoes, how would you love your neighbor?

2. In American culture, how can you tell when you are accepted as an "insider?" How does this compare to the Middle Eastern culture?

3. Compare the Middle Eastern patriarchal interpretation of the Parable of the Prodigal Son to the Western interpretation we hear in American churches. Using the Middle Eastern lens, what message do you feel Jesus was trying to drive home to the religious leaders regarding the "low-life" people they accused Jesus of hanging out with? Using the patriarchal model, what was their responsibility as symbolized by the older brother in the parable?

4. In the chapter about Bible Culture, one of the things we discussed was hospitality. In a collectivist culture, anybody that was part of your "in-group" (immediate family, extended family, clan, tribe, or fellow citizen [Israelite]) was

considered your neighbor because they were deemed safe. The Parable of the Good Samaritan (Luke 10:25-37) examines the question, "Who is my neighbor?"

   a. Using what you just learned about the prodigal son's older brother and what you learned earlier about hospitality as it relates to the in-group, what do you think Jesus was saying about the Priest's and Levite's problem in Luke 10:31-32?

   b. Considering who was supposed to be a neighbor to the in-group, what do you find so shocking about the Samaritan in Luke 10:33-35?

5. How would this Middle Eastern idea of "neighbor" translate to American culture when it comes to getting along with and fellowshipping with other Christians in your local church or other Christians who subscribe to a different belief system in another Christian denomination?

It is a Trinity

In American culture, we find it easy to express love for another person without feeling any obligation to connect emotionally with that person. Sadly, this is evidenced all too often in churches. One person says something that is offensive to another person. The other person takes offense and decides to break the relationship. At this point, unforgiveness has come to a boil on the heat of the disagreement. All the while, the aggrieved person declares, "Yes, I love that person that hurt me. I have just decided I do not want to have anything to do with them." Remember what we said earlier about the Bible words for "love" and "hate?" The apostle John wrote in 1 John 2:9 that loving involves connecting with another person. Disconnection is a problem. Isolation in the family for Middle Eastern Bible people was not tolerated under normal circumstances.

An American individualist, on the other hand, can go another direction alone and feel no guilt. This is not what the Bible conveys from its ancient Middle Eastern context. From the Bible's position, I cannot say I love another person if I remain disconnected from them.

Everywhere I look, somebody, somewhere, is glued to their cellphone. I understand that we want to stay connected with our friends, the news, the weather, and countless other things. But the connection with those who are out of our immediate presence results in disconnection from those who are right here...right now.

That is why billboards advise us on the highway, "Talk and text later." Why do we read that? Because inattention while driving can be fatal. Oh, did you say you did not see that sign? Was that because you were somehow...distracted?

What about when taking a walk or eating dinner with friends? Disconnection from the immediate present can rob me of the sights or smells of new wildflowers. It can also take from me the gift of friendship another wants to pour into my life to support and build me.

> Disconnection can be regarded as a state of being, a condition of existence where the deepest part of who we are is vibrantly attached to no one, where we are profoundly unknown and therefore experience neither the thrill of being believed in nor the joy of loving or being loved.
>
> Crabb, *Connecting: Healing for Ourselves and Our Relationships*, 44

It is interesting that Dr. Larry Crabb has linked connecting with loving and being loved. This is exactly the thrust the Bible gives in both the Old Testament and the New Testament. The Bible is not as direct about this as Dr. Crabb. The Bible merely assumes the reader knows this because this principle is an indelible part of the Bible's culture.

What mattered to the collectivist of the Bible was the strength and well-being of the group (family unit, clan, village, nation). It was the group that defined a person and gave them identity. People lived their lives outdoors. Inside was merely for sleeping, shelter, or possibly cooking. Internal feelings could only be known through external behavior toward someone else in the group.

What matters to the American is the strength or well-being of the individual ("me"). I define myself and have a good self-perception if I have good self-esteem. People in America live their lives indoors. Outside is mainly for recreation to get away from life as it is lived indoors. Internal feelings can be known and recognized without any external expression.

When an American speaks of love, one must pay attention to the context of the conversation to determine whether that internal feeling applies to food, sports, a hobby, an activity, the weather, or generally good feelings about another person. When your friend says they "love (fill in the blank)," you know you must be a detective. At this point, you probably have not seen any evidence to support their assertion. You only have clues to their internal feelings about something. You must now put these clues together to understand what your friend loves.

A Bible person was different in this regard. To love something or someone was to visibly connect with that thing or person. An external behavior announced the presence of the internal feeling. The following verses help demonstrate the difference between people of the Bible and typical Americans.

Psalm 119:159: "See how I love your precepts; preserve my life, LORD, in accordance with your love."

- Bible person: "I ("attach myself to") Your precepts";
- American: "I ("am really fond of") Your precepts";

Isaiah 43:4: "Since you are precious and honored in my sight, and because I love you, I will give people in exchange for you, nations in exchange for your life."

- Bible person: "and because I ("attach Myself to") you,"
- American: "and because I ("have a really nice feeling toward") you,"

John 3:16: "For God so loved the world that he gave his one and only Son, that whoever believes in him shall not perish but have eternal life."

- Bible person: "For God so ("attached Himself to") the world,"
- American: "For God so ("had affection for") the world,"

John 13:35: "By this everyone will know that you are my disciples, if you love one another."

- Bible person: "if you ("attach yourselves to") one another."
- American: "if you ("have nice feelings about") one another ("but you don't necessarily have to associate with them")."

From the Bible's viewpoint, loving means connecting. If the behavior of connection is not present, then the emotion of love is not present. There is a Bible word that carries the definition "walking away from." That word is "hate." While America has made progress integrating along racial lines, Christians, true followers of Jesus, have a lot of work ahead to integrate across denominational lines because of Jesus, Who reconciled us to God (2 Corinthians 5:18). Unbelievers watch us segregate ourselves into our own groups and then nit-pick other groups because they do not believe the way we believe. We really cannot say that we have a strong connection to God while we separate ourselves from another of God's children because of doctrinal beliefs (1 John 4:20). The common denominator of connection to Jesus must unite us.

What can I do when I do not "feel the love?" How do I deal with my own emotional distance while trying to make God's will for me (His child) and my difficult neighbor (also His child) a reality? Simple. I must become righteous.

You might say, "Righteousness? I thought God gave me His righteousness because Jesus took my place by dying on the cross for my sins! Why are you telling me that I still need righteousness? Didn't Jesus pay my penalty by His death?" Let us examine how the Bible describes the word "righteousness."

The earliest time in Scripture the word "righteous" or "righteousness" occurs is found in Genesis 6:9. Noah was considered righteous by God in his generation. The Hebrew word that occurs here is pronounced as [tsad-deek'] (Baker, *The Complete Word Study Dictionary: Old Testament*, H6662). The basic understanding of this word relates to conformity to a standard, a rule, or to operate within prescribed boundaries (italics mine).

Even though the word "righteous" does not occur until Genesis chapter 6, the Bible narrates how God injected His righteous character into the creation. In effect, when God designated boundaries into the created order for the Creation to follow, He actually inserted His righteousness into Creation. Here's how Genesis chapter 1 lays it out:

Day 1. Darkness and Light were divided. They now each had their own boundaries (Genesis 1:1-5).

Day 2. A vault was inserted between the waters to separate water below the expanse from the water above the expanse. The vault between the waters was called the "sky" (Genesis 1:6-8).

Day 3. The water under the expanse was gathered into one place (bounded) and called "seas." Dry land appeared. Upon the dry land, God caused to grow all manner of vegetation and fruit trees, all growing and reproducing within their own boundaries (Genesis 1:9-13).

Day 4. God set the stars and planets in the expanse above the earth ("sky," vv. 6-8). They were set for signs, sacred times, days, years, and light (Genesis 1:14-19).

Day 5. God created living creatures in the seas and birds in the heavens. Each had its own domain (bounded area). Each species was directed by God to reproduce "according to its kind" (Genesis 1:20-25).

Day 6. God created animals on the earth and mankind in a male and female variety so that they could increase upon the earth. Adam and Eve were bounded by gender (male and female), place (in a garden), and God's Word (Torah, instruction) to reproduce, have dominion over creation, and where to find food. Again, God's righteous nature is on display through boundaries (Genesis 1:26-31).

In Genesis 2, God inserted the Sabbath as Day number 7 (Genesis 2:1-3). The rest of the chapter details the process of mankind's creation, their insertion into the garden, and the boundary imposed by God's Word (Genesis 2:4-25).

Genesis chapter 3 records Eve's deception by the serpent and her transgressing (cutting across) God's verbal boundaries. It also records Adam's rebellion against

God's boundaries as well as his silence and subsequent failure to echo God's voice to Eve as a counterpoint to the serpent's deception. We know his was a silent presence because he was "with her" (Genesis 3:6). We also know his responsibility was to guard his wife against potentially harming herself, even though this responsibility was not verbalized for us until Numbers chapter 30.

Genesis chapter 4 records the uprising of violence on the earth. Cain did not guard the life of his younger brother Abel, even after being warned by God personally.

Genesis chapter 5 narrates the increase of mankind upon the earth.

By the time we get to Genesis chapter 6, violence between a man and his neighbor has reached epidemic proportions. Mankind no longer treats human life, the visible expression on earth of God's likeness and authority, as sacred. Everywhere a person looked, people were transgressing God-ordained boundaries. Righteousness seems to have been blotted out.

It is telling that God said His Spirit would not always "contend" (Genesis 6:3, [deen] in Hebrew, "to rule, judge, contend") with man (Baker, *The Complete Word Study Dictionary: Old Testament*, H1777). The picture here is, as mankind is running across God's boundary markers, God is in mankind's face, opposing man and pointing out where He has placed the boundaries. But mankind brushes God aside and pushes past Him. But there is the exception of one man, Noah. Noah observed and then heeded God's boundaries. In turn, God declared Noah righteous, a person who, like God Himself, was partial to boundaries.

What do I do when I do not "feel the love?" Observe God's boundaries concerning my neighbor. Who is my neighbor? Noah illustrates this. My closest neighbor is the "other" that lives under my roof with me. It is my wife or husband or children. While I am with them, am I the visible presence of God in their life? While I am with them, am I the audible voice of God to counter the deception of the enemy? Am I working to keep myself within God's boundaries, as He has expressed? This is righteousness in daily living. Righteousness cares how my neighbor relates to God. I do not come by myself to God. I come with my neighbor. This has nothing to do with feeling. It has everything to do with my behavior toward my neighbor before God. This is the relational love that the apostle Paul speaks to in 1 Corinthians 13. This is a love that is not self ("feelings") focused, but other ("for their benefit") focused.

How do I navigate emotional distance? I navigate that with righteousness. I navigate it by behaving within God's boundaries for the good of my neighbor. In short, I practice 1 Corinthians 13.

There is a word Christians often speak of that you will not find in the Bible. It is the word "trinity." The word "trinity" can mean either a "group of three; a triad" or the "state of being three" (Dictionary.com, "Trinity" entry).

Why is the teaching of the trinity of God important? The trinity of God is important because it gives us a working model of righteousness in action. Our Western thinking portrays "righteousness" as some far-off, philosophical idea. For most Americans, "righteousness" is something passive. "Righteousness," as defined by Americans, is a state of being that is only between an individual and God. It does not involve a relationship with another person. The American definition is worlds away from the definition used by Bible people. To them, righteous was something active. It was present only when one related positively, according to God's boundaries, to another person.

While the Bible does not specifically say anything like, "God is a Trinity," it does present snapshots that show God as One...yet Three. Here are two examples.

Deuteronomy 6:4: "Hear, O Israel: The LORD our God, the LORD is one."

Matthew 28:19: "Therefore go and make disciples of all nations, baptizing them in the name of the Father and of the Son and of the Holy Spirit, and teaching them to obey everything I have commanded you. And surely I am with you always, to the very end of the age."

We read "the LORD is one" and also read about "the Father and the Son and the Holy Spirit." In addition, we read about the close interconnectedness and attachment between the individual members of the Godhead.

John 3:35: "The Father loves the Son and has placed everything in his hands."

John 14:16: "And I will ask the Father, and he will give you another advocate to help you and be with you forever."

In the Trinity of God, we have one entity composed of three individuals cooperating and connecting in a close relationship with each other.

Would it surprise you if I told you that man is thought of in the same terms as God? God Himself declared, "Let us make mankind in our image" (Genesis 1:26). So, God brought mankind into existence in the same form that God existed. Adam was one, but three.

Again, the Bible does not specifically state, "Man is a Trinity." Instead, the Bible presents snapshots that theologians arrange into a photo album called "theology." Consider the following Scripture passages. Scripture speaks of man's body (physical being), spirit or soul (spiritual being), and mind (intellect). Following are two examples.

Proverbs 20:27: "The human spirit is the lamp of the LORD that sheds light on one's inmost being."

1 Thessalonians 5:23: "May God himself, the God of peace, sanctify you through and through. May your whole spirit, soul and body be kept blameless at the coming of our Lord Jesus Christ."

God is presented in Scripture as somewhat like a prism. A prism is a single object having three sides. When light travels through a prism, the prism bends the light so that its various facets, or colors, may be seen. God is One but Three. As man was made in the "likeness of God" (Genesis 1:26), Man is also one but three. The three parts of man have a single purpose: to act and be as a single individual.

The three parts of man must "love" (connect in close relationship to) each other for there to be life. If the body and the soul are separated, life ceases. If a man "loses his mind," meaningful life in the community ceases because the man enters a vegetative state.

The "church" is not a building. It is a collective of people, a creation of God. God has always had individuals distinguished by their unique relationship with God. Jesus declared in Matthew 16:18, "And I tell you that you are Peter, and on this rock I will build my church, and the gates of Hades will not overcome it."

Two other verses in the Book of Acts discuss "the church" in terms of a group of people gathered together, unified by God's name and purpose.

Acts 12:5: "So Peter was kept in prison, but the church was earnestly praying to God for him."

Acts 14:27: "On arriving there, they gathered the church together and reported all that God had done through them and how he had opened a door of faith to the Gentiles."

As with God and with God's partner, man, the church is a Trinity. When one speaks of the "church," there is an understanding that one speaks of God, the person (or individual) related to God, and that person's "neighbor" (the "other" person within the wider group known as the "church"). The word "church" presupposes a three-dimensional reality. If I am only thinking of "just me and Jesus," I am not thinking about the "church," otherwise known as "the body of Christ." "Jesus and me" does not comprise the "church." Scripture speaks of more than a dyad (me and Jesus). In Scripture, there is a supposition of at least a triad (me, Jesus, and my neighbor). The apostle Paul put it this way.

> Just as a body, though one, has many parts, but all its many parts form one body, so it is with Christ. For we were all baptized by one Spirit so as to form one body—whether

Jews or Gentiles, slave or free—and we were
all given the one Spirit to drink. Even so the
body is not made up of one part but of many.

1 Corinthians 12:12-14

Man, with one hand, reaches to God. But what does
a man do with his other hand? God made humans with
two hands! Humans reach for God with one hand and
reach for their neighbor with the other hand.

Within the Body of Christ, we each have the responsibility of focusing not on ourselves and what we want,
but rather on the Head, Christ, and what He wants happening in the Body.

Without the Head, Christ, the church is dead. Without my neighbor, another member of the Body, the
church is dead.

God has attached Himself to ("loves") the Son. The
Father, the Son, and the Holy Spirit work cooperatively
together.

Man's Spirit, mind, and body are inseparable. Each
part of man is interconnected and cooperates fully, creating an individual who is vibrantly alive.

For the health and life of His people, God has created a triad (a trinity) called the church. As I have been
brought into fellowship with God, God also expects me
and my Christian neighbor to work out our differences
so that we can show the world what God is like. Jesus

expects me to attach myself to my neighbor. If I refuse a relationship with my Christian neighbor, I cannot call myself a Christian because I am walking in darkness (1 John 2:9). To sever my relationship with my Christian neighbor is to sever my relationship with Jesus. Jesus told us plainly in John 13:35, "By this everyone will know that you are my disciples, if you love one another." The only way we can walk with Jesus is if we commit to walking in solidarity with our neighbor, our brother or sister in Christ. If we refuse, we are not Christian. We are only religious.

Questions for Group Reflection

1. In the section above detailing the relationship between "loving" and "connecting," the statement is made, "We really cannot say that we have a strong connection to God while we separate ourselves from another of God's children because of doctrinal beliefs (1 John 4:20)." Discuss in your group how you feel about that statement. Do your conclusions support a Western or Middle Eastern understanding? Is your answer closer to the Bible or closer to American culture?

2. Why do you feel established boundaries are important for relationships to work well? What is the function of boundaries? How do you think boundaries we have erected because of denominational differences have hindered our relating as Jesus followers?

3. Discuss the statement: "Without the Head, Christ, the church is dead. Without my neighbor, another member of the Body, the church is dead."

4. How would you diagnose the spiritual health of a Christian group (church or small group) that is experiencing a lot of division? If you were the "spiritual doctor," what would that group need to do to regain spiritual health?

5. Read John 13:35. How is that verse often understood in American (Western) churches? Now, apply the Middle Eastern understanding of "love" to this verse. How does this shift how you would live this out in your Christian group?

Roadside Repair
When the Wheels
Fall Off

It was going to be an all-day trip. We were traveling in our Chevrolet station wagon about 473 kilometers (almost 300 miles) from Natitingou, Benin, West Africa, to Ouagadougou, Burkina Faso, West Africa. Adding time for lunch, you could count on an eight and a half to nine and a half hour trip. It was all dirt road. There were no gas stations or rest stops. There were no restaurants or fast-food restaurants. Just dirt road that snaked through the African savannah.

We had completed most of the journey when an awful, grinding, metal-against-metal screeching sound began. It was not long before the car lost power, and we coasted to the side of the road. It was hot! The late afternoon sun gave no relief, and there was no shade tree in sight. I was a child, but I still remember the feeling I had in the pit of my stomach. I felt helpless and afraid. I was thirsty. Most of all, I was fearful of not reaching the safety of our destination, the neighboring mission station.

Dad, an excellent mechanic, got out of the car and went to inspect the damage. I saw the very thing he did. There was one rear wheel, axle-attached, that was almost out of the rear wheel well. The wheel bearing had failed and seized. This allowed the rear wheel and axle to separate from the differential. The engine ran fine, but we were not going anywhere, and it was clear Dad could not fix it. We were really stuck!

We had no phones. There were no welcome signs of a gas station or motel. There was no one to appeal to for help. Our only option was to wait and hope that someone else traveling in our direction would give us a ride. After a long wait, a Frenchman happened along. He loaded our family into his Peugeot and took us to our destination. We would actually eat supper and enjoy a good night's sleep! Dad would get the help he needed from our host missionary. We would conclude our business and get home.

A community of Christians is often called a "family." As individuals join together, in a common bond, for the common good, going in the same direction, they often resemble a family unit. There is a leader or leaders who steer the course. There are some who are along for the adventure. There are others who wonder about their comfort on the journey. Some may even be resistant to the route chosen by the driver or mode of transportation. You can sometimes see this last group with arms folded or hear them muttering under their breath. There is one thing, however, you can count on. Everybody wants to arrive at the same destination. Doesn't that sound like a church or small group?

Invariably as the group is traveling, something happens that causes the group to lose power. Sometimes the breakdown is quiet and individual members leave the group. Sometimes the separation is accompanied by loud accusations and angry dissent. Either way, you are stuck on the side of the road.

Relational wheels are fragile. They tend to break at the weakest point. I find it interesting that my weakest point always seems to be where my wants and comfort grind against someone else's needs or demands. It may be God saying in His Word, "Go this way," when I want to go "that way." It can also be the need of another member of the group that grates against my plans for comfort. If I do not reflect on where I am with the Lord or with my neighbor, I end up coming undone. That causes the group problems. We then find ourselves stuck by the side of the road until we can find a solution.

There is one main way that a discipleship group differs from a Sunday School or Catechism class. Whenever I have attended (in my Christian journey) a Sunday School class, I have found that I was able to come and go without getting dirty. Information was free for the taking. The information went in one ear...and took up residence in my brain. Rarely did it filter the eighteen inches to my heart! How did that happen? I was not getting my hands dirty. If you want to fix something that is broken, expect to get your hands dirty. You will need to do some digging, some uncovering, and some replacing in order to get up and be running again.

Why is this so hard? The problem, I believe, is not that the work needs to be done. The problem lies in the expectations brought into this community of Christians. Outward expectations (designed to preserve one's image in the group) suggest that there are no weak areas. Everything is fine! We are all brand new off the showroom floor. Every part of us begins this journey meeting or exceeding all manufactures' recommendations. We could not be any better and certainly need no improvement (tongue in cheek)!

There is something I did not mention to you about that Chevrolet station wagon. Our family was the second owner. The previous owner had hit a dump-truck load of dirt in bad visibility at night. That collision caused a great amount of front-end damage and some engine damage. The car needed extensive work before we could use it. Dad was the engine and drive-train mechanic as well as the body shop technician. When he was finished, we had transportation that was superior to the cramped cab of our 1956 Chevrolet pickup. We could spread out and enjoy the ride. My point is this: when we got the car, it was a broken car. This is an important point to consider when joining a discipleship group. Nobody comes in off the showroom floor. We have all had our share of rough roads, and most of them were not paved! If the stories were told, we would find that we have all experienced collisions with life that left us wounded and disabled. We are all in need of God's restoration!

The more inflated a person becomes with pride, the higher they soar. The higher a person rises, the farther they must fall. I must be honest here. I would much rather step off the front step out my front door to the ground than get to the ground suddenly off the roof! The higher you go, the easier it is to reach terminal velocity. Do I want to experience a slight bump or a hard fall? Hit the ground the wrong way, and a fall off the roof could be fatal! (And now you know why skydiving is not my recreation of choice!)

Since we are on this discipleship journey as a threesome (me, God, and my neighbor), the case for humility needs examination. We will begin with some Scripture.

Isaiah 57:15: "For this is what the high and exalted One says—he who lives forever, whose name is holy: 'I live in a high and holy place, but also with the one who is contrite and lowly in spirit, to revive the spirit of the lowly and to revive the heart of the contrite.'"

Micah 6:8: "He has shown you, O mortal, what is good. And what does the LORD require of you? To act justly and to love mercy and to walk humbly with your God."

Job 22:29: "When people are brought low and you say, 'Lift them up!' then he will save the downcast."

Matthew 18:4: "Therefore, whoever takes the lowly position of this child is the greatest in the kingdom of heaven."

James 4:6: "But he gives us more grace. That is why Scripture says: 'God opposes the proud but shows favor to the humble.'"

Colossians 3:12: "Therefore, as God's chosen people, holy and dearly loved, clothe yourselves with compassion, kindness, humility, gentleness and patience.

1 Peter 5:5: "In the same way, you who are younger, submit yourselves to your elders. All of you, clothe yourselves with humility toward one another, because, "God opposes the proud but shows favor to the humble."

Ephesians 4:1-2: "As a prisoner for the Lord, then, I urge you to live a life worthy of the calling you have received. Be completely humble and gentle; be patient, bearing with one another in love."

When we observe these Scripture notations relating to the subject of humility, we can make the following conclusions:

1. Even though God's throne (authority, power, and provision) is high above all that is in the heavens and on earth, God personally practices humility (Isaiah 57:15).
2. God's desire for mankind is that people also practice humility (Micah 6:8).
3. God attends to (or saves) the humble person and exalts that person (Job 22:29; Matthew 18:4).
4. If a person lives in pride, that person stands in opposition to God (James 4:6).
5. All those who align themselves with God are to "clothe themselves with" humility (Colossians 3:12; 1 Peter 5:5).

Now, why didn't I discuss Ephesians 4:1-2 with the other verses? Well, that is because it forms the concluding instructions on how to make a relational repair on the side of the road when the wheels fall off.

When it comes to dealing with people with whom I am out-of-sorts, it helps when there is somebody at your side, coaching you on how to get things fixed and running again. This time it is the apostle Paul.

When you are scratching your head as you survey the damage, the apostle Paul comes to your side with his toolbox of Ephesians 4:1-2. I think his instructions might sound something like this from Ephesians 4:2:

1. "First, pick up that wrench of humility. Humility is going to loosen things up a bit so that you can get to the real problems causing your difficulty.
2. "Use gentleness here. That bolt is pretty worn, so you will need to ease it loose.
3. "Remember, as you are applying humility to this situation, things will not necessarily loosen up immediately. You will need both patience and persistence with this. This might take a while. I know this is hard, but you've got this!
4. "As that bolt loosens, you may hear some squeaking. The noise you hear is feedback from the bolt because it was torqued down too tight. You must listen to that feedback and not dismiss what the bolt is telling you. This is called 'tolerance.' The reason we need tolerance is that this is a learning situation. It is a good thing you have the wrench of humility in your hand! That is the only wrench that can get into this tight spot in a learning situation!
5. "Finally, remember why you are doing all this. This is no time for you to kick the tire and walk

away from this repair. You are broken down by the side of the road because one small piece has failed. Every single part of this vehicle has its own breaking point. This time it was the bolt. Next time it might be the air filter or the wiper blade. The fact that failure happened does not matter. What matters is that you need every part of this vehicle to get you to your destination. That means you need to attach yourself to (love) this vehicle because it is your only ride home. You cannot get home by yourself."

Remember, stuff happens. There is no perfect group or situation. How can that be? I am not perfect. Neither is anybody else in the group. We are all broken at some point and have our rough places. The sooner we can put on the character qualities that can bring healing, the sooner we can get going again...together.

Questions for Group Reflection

1. Consider the nature of American (Western) culture. Why do you think Christian group dynamics are often fragile? Discuss what you think competes against the cohesiveness, solidarity, and well-being of many Christian groups.

2. Consider how Americans seek to be masters of their environment. This is one of the foundation stones of an "individualist." How does this cultural driving force counter the Bible's call for humility? Discuss how we can become more sensitive to God's call and counter a culture that pulls us away from God's instructions for living.

3. Read John 15:5. Discuss how this runs contrary to the American cultural message that celebrates self-reliance. How can we become more sensitive to the message of Jesus? Discuss how we can grow deeper in Jesus in this area while living in our deviant culture.

4. Discuss the difference between a Christian church culture that focuses on "I am fine/you are fine" versus a Christian church culture that accepts individual brokenness as a starting point (like Alcoholics Anonymous). Which do you think is a more accurate Christian model and why? Discuss what prevents Christians from uniting in brokenness and joining together for mutual healing.

Getting Across the Finish Line

Discipleship is a program that unites people of varied backgrounds under a common cause: learning to be like Jesus. Age does not matter. Status does not matter. Occupation does not matter. This program crosses racial boundaries. It crosses country borders. It even cuts across denominational lines. There is a common thread that unites us. The man born blind in John 9:25 put it this way, "I was blind, but now I see." We all have common brokenness, sin, now dealt with by the death and resurrection of Jesus. We all have a common purpose. God gave us our destiny written in Romans 8:29. God's purpose is for us to become conformed to the likeness of Jesus. God destined our character to become like His. We are united. We are all in this together.

As we are traveling together, it is easy to get impatient with the journey. Children, by nature, want things as soon as they experience the need...now. Patience only comes with maturity and experience. This is the reason why traveling with young children can be challenging. "Are we there yet?" is the question often heard by parents driving some distance so the children can visit their grandparents.

This experience of traveling with children is sometimes replicated in either young Christians or Christians who have not yet had a lot of experience with discipleship. I have been guilty of this thinking mistake myself. What thinking mistake, you ask? The thinking I am referring to is the assumption that once I master this thing called "discipleship," I can move on to something else.

This faulty understanding presupposes that discipleship is a class that a person takes. This thinking mistake is that discipleship has a defined starting date and a defined ending date. A person begins their discipleship journey when they start the class and learn all they need to know by the end of class. At the conclusion of the class, a person's thinking might be something like this, *Well, I have finished that. What do I take next?* In other words, once a person finishes learning about discipleship, they are ready to tackle another project.

Discipleship is not a trip to your grandparents' house once a year. It is a lifetime of living as a person who is in fellowship with other Believers and the Lord Jesus. Discipleship is not a class.

We begin discipleship when we commit our lives to the Lord Jesus and come under His authority. Some call this "conversion." Others call this "salvation." Jesus called it being "born again" (John 3:3). He also called it being "born of the Spirit" (John 3:8). Graduation from discipleship is the moment we enter heaven by way of either death or what the Bible describes as being "caught up" to meet the Lord in the air (1 Thessalonians 4:17). In short, the walking out of discipleship after conversion is a lifetime commitment. We cannot quantify "there" when we are tempted to ask the question, "Are we there yet?" God, as we walk with Him, continually reveals to us areas of our lives that need transforming. This could be anything in the areas of behavior (body) or emotions and thinking (spirit/mind). Anybody who rubs up against this world order will get scuff marks. These blemishes to the Christian shine must be buffed out through the transformation process. We all will have opportunities to learn how to behave like Jesus behaved. We all will have opportunities to think about life, God, and our neighbor like Jesus thought. Discipleship is not industrial-strength Christianity applied to the home-variety Christian. Discipleship is the normal Christian experience. Discipleship is your garden-variety Christianity applied to all us "regular" Christians.

Since the practice of discipleship is a life-long adventure with Jesus, what do we do from now until we cross the finish line? We continue growing deeper in Jesus. My wife and I knew a couple several years ago, one of whom worked for the County Sheriff's Department. Every so often, she was required to requalify on the firing range. This was a normal part of her job. She carried a weapon. To my knowledge, she never needed to discharge her weapon in the line of her duty. Still, she was required to prove competency on a regular basis in the basics. To succeed at her job overall, she had to practice the basics.

When Vince Lombardi took over the Green Bay Packers in the late 1950s, he took over a losing football team that had learned to lose, was okay with losing, and often gave up in a game. Lombardi did not clean house and get new players on his team. He transformed the players he had. He used a military-style discipline. He cajoled and congratulated. He never quit seeing the great potential each of those players had. He did make some position changes. He did develop some new plays to keep the opposing team's defense guessing. Most of all, Lombardi drilled the basics of football until they became second nature. The losing players were transformed from a losing team to a record of 7:5 Lombardi's first year. Lombardi went on to create a football dynasty. Quarterback Bart Starr was one of those players (Baker, "A Look Back at How Vince Lombardi Launched a Dynasty," 2010).

Practicing the basics of Bible study, prayer, and relating well to (loving) my neighbor is essential to growing a Christian life. These are the basics of discipleship.
Yes, a person can later bring in other disciplines like
fasting, solitude, simplicity, celebration, or helping the
poor as disciplines that enrich the Christian life. Whatever one does, wherever one serves, one must remember one thing. The strength of the foundation deter-
mines the stability of the structure. If the foundation
of a house shifts or cracks, the superstructure that rests
on the foundation soon has visible problems. North
Texas is notorious for having shifting clay soil. Visible
signs of foundation problems are cracks in the ceilings
or walls or doors that stick or will not shut. If the foundation is not stable, the rest of the house is in trouble.

Discipleship is like that. We must attend to the basics. We must practice the basics until they become
second nature. If a person slides away from these
foundational elements, it will not take long before others notice cracks that just do not look like Jesus. If left
unaddressed, these will worsen over time. What is the
solution? Repair the foundation of Bible study, prayer,
and walking in solidarity with one's neighbor. This
is called repentance. Keep tending to the basics, and
watch how, over time, Jesus transforms you from having a losing record to a winning one!

Questions for Group Reflection

1. Reflect for a moment on why you think people divide. When people get polarized, what do you think they are focusing on? What do you think they want? To a polarized person, who is "the enemy?" Now, look at John 10:10 and discuss who the enemy is. Compare with Ephesians 6:12.

2. When we join ourselves with others, somebody, sometime, is sure to "spill their milk." At that moment, we feel anger or frustration. Using Genesis 1-6 as a backdrop (the story culminating with "righteous" Noah), discuss how we might navigate these rapids of emotional distance so we can get back into harmony.

3. Why do you think it is so difficult to move from a place of disunity to a place of harmony? Consider James 4:6 and 1 Peter 5:5. Why do you think humility is a place where we find the power and the presence of God? Look at Isaiah 57:15. What does this verse contribute to our discussion? What do you think this verse says about God's character quality of humility? If you have never thought about God being humble, you might look again at Philippians 2:3-11.

4. One of the common denominators of 12-step addiction recovery groups (like Alcoholics Anony-

mous) is the mutual bond of brokenness. "Hi. My name is Bob, and I am an alcoholic." This is the kind of greeting you hear at one of these gatherings. Compare this to what we often find at church gatherings. Now, discuss how a spirit of humility that sees another's brokenness and empathizes with that brokenness can promote unity and healing in church gatherings. Where do pride and humility figure in?

5. When things do not get better quickly, we tend to get impatient. Reflect on what the source of that impatience might be. Now, discuss what bearing James 1:2-5 might have on this discussion. What character quality do you think God might be trying to develop? What character of God do you see in 2 Peter 3:9? How does all this relate to Romans 12:2?

Endnotes

1. American Bible Society, Barna Group, "State of the Bible 2019." Report of the research conducted January 15 through February 7, 2019: 3, 6, https://www.americanbible.org/uploads/content/state-of-the-bible-2019_report_041619_final.pdf.

2 Ted Vanlandeghem, "Jewish Marriage Customs" (part of the Jewish Seder presentation and explanation at Capstone Church, Benbrook, Easter weekend), April 2019.

3 Eugene H. Peterson, *Christ Plays in Ten Thousand Places: A Conversation in Spiritual Theology.* (Grand Rapids, Michigan: William B. Eerdmans Publishing Company, 2005), 1.

Bibliography

Andrews, Robin George. "Coronavirus Turns Urban Life's Roar to Whisper on World's Seismographs." Posted April 8, 2020. *The New York Times*, https://www.nytimes.com/2020/04/08/science/seismographs-lockdown-coronavirus.html.

Baker, C. Douglas. "A Look Back at How Vince Lombardi Launched a Dynasty." Posted July 3, 2010. *Bleacher Report*, https://bleacherreport.com/articles/415144-a-look-back-at-how-vince-lombardi-launched-a-dynasty.

Baker, Warren, D.R.E. and Eugene Carpenter, PhD, *The Complete Word Study Dictionary: Old Testament*. Chattanooga: AMG Publishers, 2003.

Bivin, David. *New Light on the Difficult Words of Jesus: Insights from His Jewish Context*. Holland, MI. En-Gedi Resource Center, Inc. 2005.

Carson, D. A. "Matthew." *The Expositor's Bible Commentary: Matthew, Mark, Luke*, edited by F. E. Gaebelein.

Vol. 8, 194. Grand Rapids, MI: Zondervan Publishing House, 1984.

Coley, Michael. Bible Reading.com. 2009 (online and printable format), http://www.bible-reading.com/ bible-plan.html.

Crabb, Larry. *Connecting: Healing for Ourselves and Our Relationships*. Nashville: W. Publishing Group, 1997.

Crystal Park Baptist Church, Benoni, South Africa. "Category: Spurgeon," 2020, https://www.crystalpark-baptistchurch.co.za/category/spurgeon/page/2/.

deSilva, David A. *Honor, Patronage, Kinship & Purity*. Madison, WI: InterVarsity Press, 2000.

Dictionary.com, s.v. "theology" entry, https://www.dictionary.com/browse/theology?s=t.

Dictionary.com, s.v. "Trinity" entry, https://www.dictionary.com/browse/Trinity?s=t.

Foster, Richard J. *Celebration of Discipline*. New York: HarperCollins Publishers, 1978.

Hertz, Dr. Joseph H. *The Authorized Daily Prayer Book*. New York: Bloch Publishing Company, 1948.

Kidd, Thomas. "What 'Deist' Meant to Thomas Jefferson," TGC (Blog), The Gospel Coalition: U.S. Edition, July 8, 2020, https://www.thegospelcoalition.org/blogs/evangelical-history/ what-deist-meant-to-thomas-jefferson/.

Lieber, Rabbi Moshe. *The Pirkei Avos Treasury / Ethics of the Fathers: The Sages' Guide to Living with an Antholo-*

gized Commentary and Anecdotes, edited by Rabbi Nosson Scherman. Brooklyn: Mesorah Publications, Ltd., 1995.

Malina, Bruce J. and Jerome H. Neyrey. "Honor and Shame in Luke-Acts: Pivotal Values of the Mediterranean World." *The Social World of Luke-Acts*, edited by Jerome H. Neyrey, 25-65. Peabody, MS: Hendrickson Publishers, Inc., 1991.

Malina, Bruce J. and Chris Seaman. "Envy." *Handbook of Biblical Social Values*, edited by John J. Pilch and Bruce J. Malina, 59–63. Peabody, MS: Hendrickson Publishers, Inc., 1993.

Malina, Bruce J. "Love." *Handbook of Biblical Social Values*, edited by John J. Pilch and Bruce J. Malina, 127–130. Peabody, MS: Hendrickson Publishers, Inc., 1993.

Malina, Bruce J. "Hospitality." *Handbook of Biblical Social Values*, edited by John J. Pilch and Bruce J. Malina, 115–118. Peabody, MS: Hendrickson Publishers, Inc., 1993.

Malina, Bruce J. *The New Testament World: Insights from Cultural Anthropology*. Louisville: John Knox Press, 1993.

Malina, Bruce J. *Social Science Commentary on the Synoptic Gospels*. Minneapolis: Augsburg Fortress Press, 1992.

Malina, Bruce J. and Richard L. Rohrbaugh. *Social-Science Commentary on the Gospel of John*. Minneapolis: Fortress Press, 1998.

Merriam-Webster.com Dictionary, s.v. "deism" entry, https://www.merriam-webster.com/dictionary/deism.

Nee, Watchman. *Spiritual Authority*. New York: Christian Fellowship Publishers, Inc., 1972.

Neyrey, Jerome H., SJ, and Richard L. Rohrbaugh. "He Must Increase, I Must Decrease (John 3:30): A Cultural and Social Interpretation." *The Social World of the New Testament: Insights and Models*, edited by Jerome H. Neyrey and Eric C. Stewart, 237–251. Peabody, MS: Hendrickson Publishers, Inc., 2008.

Neyrey, Jerome H. and Eric C. Stewart. "Economics." *The Social World of the New Testament: Insights and Models*, edited by Jerome H. Neyrey and Eric C. Stewart, 63. Peabody, MS: Hendrickson Publishers, Inc., 2008.

Peterson, Eugene H. *Christ Plays In Ten Thousand Places*. Grand Rapids: Wm. B. Eerdmans Publishing Co., 2005.

Pilch, John J. *A Cultural Handbook to the Bible*. Grand Rapids: Wm. B. Eerdmans Publishing Co., 2012.

Pilch, John J. "Altruism (Almsgiving)." *Handbook of Biblical Social Values*, edited by John J. Pilch & Bruce J. Malina, 8–10. Peabody, MS: Hendrickson Publishers, Inc., 1993.

Pilch, John J. "Emotion/Demonstration of Feelings." *Handbook of Biblical Social Values*, edited by John J.

Pilch & Bruce J. Malina, 56–59. Peabody, MS: Hendrickson Publishers, Inc., 1993.

Pilch, John J. "Compassion." *Handbook of Biblical Social Values*, edited by John J. Pilch & Bruce J. Malina, 30–33. Peabody, MS: Hendrickson Publishers, Inc., 1993.

Plevnik, Joseph. "Honor/Shame." *Handbook of Biblical Social Values*, edited by John J. Pilch & Bruce J. Malina, 106–115. Peabody, MS: Hendrickson Publishers, Inc., 1993.

Quote Investigator. "Give a Man a Fish, and You Feed Him for a Day. Teach a Man to Fish, and You Feed Him for a Lifetime," August 8, 2015, https://quoteinvestigator.com/2015/08/28/fish.

Richards, E. Randolph and Brandon J. O'Brien. *Misreading Scripture With Western Eyes: Removing Cultural Blinders to Better Understand the Bible*. Downers Grove, IL: IVP Books, 2012.

Riggleman, Heather. Christianity.com, "Who Were the Major and Minor Prophets of the Bible?" Originally published September 16, 2019, https://www.christianity.com/wiki/bible/who-were-the-major-and-minor-prophets-in-the-bible.html.

Rohrbaugh, Richard L. *The New Testament in Cross-Cultural Perspective*. Eugene, OR: Wipf and Stock Publishers, a division of Cascade Books, 2007.

Rose Publishing. *Bible Overview*. (printed by the publisher as both an e-book and also pamphlet – ISBN-

13: 9781890947712). Torrance, CA: Rose Publishing, 2004.

Siegler, MG, Techcrunch, "Eric Schmidt: Every 2 Days We Create As Much Information As We Did Up To 2003," posted August 4, 2010, https://techcrunch.com/2010/08/04/schmidt-data/.

Tverberg, Lois with Bruce Okkema. *Listening to the Language of the Bible: Hearing it Through Jesus' Ears*. Holland, MI: En-Gedi Resource Center, Inc., 2004.

Vander Laan, Ray. "Israel's Mission with Ray Vander Laan Session One." Directed by John Grooters, performed by Ray Vander Laan: Grooters Productions. Focus on the Family/Zondervan, 2015. https://www.youtube.com/watch?v=Dm7S101cyJM.

Walton, John H. *Ancient Near Eastern Thought and the Old Testament: Introducing the Conceptual World of the Hebrew Bible*. Grand Rapids: Baker Academic, 2006.

Walton, John H. "Interpreting the Creation Story." Seven-Minute Seminary. Streamed live on April 22, 2015. YouTube video. https://www.youtube.com/watch?v=lKWVPVp_GZQ.

Wikipedia, s.v. "Watchman Nee" entry, last modified 4 November 2020, https://en.wikipedia.org/wiki/Watchman_Nee.

Wilson, Marvin R. *Our Father Abraham: Jewish Roots of the Christian Faith*. Grand Rapids: Wm. B. Eerdmans Publishing Company, 1989.

Worldometer. "COVID-19 Coronavirus Pandemic," accessed April 11, 2020, https://www.worldometers. info/coronavirus/.

Zlotowitz, Rabbi Meir. *Bereishis / Genesis: A New Translation With a Commentary Anthologized from Talmudic, Midrashic and Rabbinic Sources.* Vol. 1a. New York: Mesorah Publications, Ltd., 1977.

Author Bio

Larry Metz was raised by missionary parents in West Africa. Growing up in a bicultural (American and West African) setting intrigued Larry from an early age. Finding many similarities between African culture and the Middle Eastern culture of the Bible, Larry became curious to discover more about Biblical culture. Larry earned his MA in Biblical Studies from Evangel University in Springfield, Missouri, after completing his BA in Religious Education. In business, Larry has worked in retail sales and sales tax accounting. In ministry, Larry has served as an assistant pastor (Minister of Education), pastor, and Christian School Administrator. He has also completed six units of Clinical Pastoral Education (CPE) in a hospital chaplaincy setting. Larry is ordained by Chaplaincy of Full Gospel Churches. Larry and his wife, Kathy, live in Fort Worth, Texas. They have two adult sons and three grandchildren.

CPSIA information can be obtained
at www.ICGtesting.com
Printed in the USA
BVHW080037070721
611238BV00016B/864

9 781637 690963